Alan Williams is a thriller-writer and journalist who has travelled all over the world gathering material for this book. Maggie Noach is a literary agent and co-editor of *The Romantic Weekend Book*

The Dictionary of Disgusting Facts

Alan Williams and Maggie Noach

Futura

A Futura Book

Copyright © Alan Williams and Maggie Noach 1986
Foreword copyright © 1986 Barry Humphries

First published in 1986
by Futura Publications, a Division of
Macdonald & Co (Publishers) Ltd
London & Sydney

ISBN 0 7088 2888 4

Printed and bound in Great Britain by
Hazell, Watson & Viney Ltd.,
Aylesbury, Bucks

Futura Publications
A Division of
Macdonald & Co (Publishers) Ltd
Maxwell House
74 Worship Street
London EC2A 2EN

A BPCC plc Company

Contents

Lichen	Scalping
Lick eczema	Self-immolation
Lithopaedion	Semen
Liver	Sewage
Lupus	Sex aids
Masturbation	Sexual intercourse
Meat baths	Shrunken heads
Mendicants	Smegma
Menstruation	Snakes
Mercury poisoning	Snot
Mould	Sootikin
Necrophilia	Spermatazoa
Nose-picking	Spitting
Obesity	Strangulated hernia
Oral sex	Syphilis
Oriental sore	Tapeworm
Ovarian cysts	Tattooing
Palang	Teratoma tumour
Penis	Testicles
Perspiration	Thrush
Pet preservation	Trans-sexualism
Pharaoh's ants	Trepanation
Piercing	Urination
Piles	Urine therapy
Placenta	Vagina
Plague	Vaginismus
Plaque	Varicose veins
Psoriasis	Vomit
Pubic hair	Water
Purgatives	Webbed fingers and toes
Rats	Weil's Disease
Rejuvenation	Women (inflatable)
Round-worm	troops for the use of
Saliva	Zits
Scaldrum dodge	Zoonoses

Acknowledgements

We are grateful for permission to reproduce copyright material from:

Brian W. Aldiss: *The Eighty-Minute Hour*, published by Jonathan Cape Ltd, reprinted by permission of the author.

Beverley Cross: *Mars in Capricorn*, published by Rupert Hart-Davis, copyright © Beverley Cross 1955, reprinted by permission of Curtis Brown Ltd.

Tom Driberg: *Ruling Passions*, published by Jonathan Cape Ltd, reprinted by permission of David Higham Associates Ltd.

Daphne Fielding: *The Face on the Phoenix* and David Niven: *The Moon's A Balloon*, reprinted by permission of Hamish Hamilton Ltd.

Many people helped in our research. We would particularly like to thank Barry Humphries, alias Sir Les Patterson, and Brian Aldiss.

FOREWORD BY
DR SIR LESLIE COLIN PATTERSON

Being an Australian elder statesman from way back, I am no stranger to disgusting facts. If you don't believe me, sit on any heated debate in Parliament House, Canberra, and you will listen to more disgusting facts in five minutes than a moll would hear in a life-time at the knock-shop.

I'm a frank, up-front type of bloke, so I freely admit now, I haven't read this publication that I am writing an intro for, except that it sounds on the educational side. Let's face it, life is not all a bed of roses and very rarely does it smell like one.

I'd be a hypocrite if I told you I've always managed to keep my nose clean over a lifetime in Aussie politics. It's not for nothing my favourite classical tune is 'Colonel Bogie'.

I've knocked around the diplomatic traps in some pretty off-beat nooks and crannies of this planet, and I reckon if I wrote a publication about some of the things I've seen, I would have to pinch the title of this book.

But there are mollycoddled kids being brought up in the world today by rat-bag parents who are protected from some of life's more earthy and sometimes delightful experiences. Result: they go berserk at 45 and rape their mothers-in-law – *and that's if they're lucky.*

'A peck of dirt is good for you' was a wise old saying of my father's before he passed away quietly in his sleep one day between the bar and the gents, and my spies tell me there is more than a peck of dirt in the pages of this informative volume.

For my sins I am Chairman of the Cheese Board and I have to attend umpteen cheese sniffings per week. Distinguishing between a fine old Tasmanian mauve vein and an Ayres Roquefort in a state of tertiary fermentation requires a finely tuned hooter, and Les Patterson's nose is famous in sniffing circles. That's why I keep the king-size mentholateds down to a minimum before breakfast, and I never cat on an empty stomach.

My love of cheese has taught me to distinguish between a few other organic pongs, and I wonder if our authors in their research have given you the lowdown on sebum (See Acne) and smegma? And I really mean the lowdown in the case of these two popular serbacious secretions (scrabble players will know what I'm talking about here).

I hope this learned work will find its way into schools, parliamentary cloakrooms, and the odd nunnery. It ought to teach you a lot about the nature of man because, let's face it, you may think you know a person but the real real bloke is underneath his fingernails.

God bless Australia!

Leslie Colin Patterson, Ph.D (Hons, Cambridge), K.C.B.E.

Australian Cultural Attaché to the Court of St. James

Emeritus Professor of London School of Antipodean Studies

Chairman of the Australian Bicentennial Cheese Board

Federal Minister for the Yartz

Introduction

Many subjects excite a morbid, even repellant, fascination which for most of us remains sadly ungratified. The authors of this book have spent many hours combing obscure medical and legal tomes, tracking down experts in such arcane matters as fartleberries and cannibalism, asking questions which the majority of people would never have dared think about, let alone put into words.

Have you not always longed to know more about trepanation; the ingredients of budgerigar casserole; and the true reason why two Very Important People were asked to leave a smart Sussex hotel at *very* short notice in the summer of 1948? Years of exhaustive research by the authors now reveal the answers to these and many other questions you never thought of asking. Everything in this book is true.

This is *not* the ideal Christmas present for your Great Aunt – or has she, too, a secret curiosity for all those disgusting facts of life and death which hold such relentless fascination for even the most squeamish?

Abattoir

The air of an abattoir – or slaughter-house – is pungent with the stench of blood and offal, mingled with the screams of fear; imminent death communicates itself to dumb animals as surely as to a condemned man when the judge puts on the black cap.

During the Algerian War, the French Army discovered an abattoir-with-a-difference during a search on the border of the French and Arab quarters of Oran. The hooks along the ceiling were hung not with the carcasses of freshly-slain animals but with dead Europeans. Reports rapidly spread through the terrified French population that the Algerian Liberation Army – many of them Muslims who were reluctant to give their own blood – had hit on the idea of kidnapping French civilians and draining off their blood for transfusions to the wounded. After the area had been sealed off, a French officer told one of the authors: 'I have seen things in there I will never forget.'

Because the French government was anxious to unload itself of the Algerian problem, all reports of this atrocity were either suppressed or rigorously denied. The author's own report, published in a London newspaper, prompted both the Algerian *and* French authorities to complain about him; no mean achievement since the two countries had been at war for more than seven years!

Abscess

An accumulation of pus which develops rapidly around infected wounds, caused by the invasion of bacteria (*qv*). These are attacked by white corpuscles in the blood which collect around the invaded area and attempt to destroy the bacteria, either by devouring and digesting them or by forming anti-bacterial substances. Pus itself consists of dead bacteria and white corpuscles which have undergone fatty degeneration. It is nature's way of dealing with infection but the accumulation of too much pus can cause an abscess to burst.

The film director John Irvin recalls that one of his camera-men on location in the Yemeni Desert had a large lump on his arm. It grew rapidly, causing irritation but gave him little pain, until it burst and a perfectly-formed abscess the size and texture of a soft-boiled hen's egg popped out. Inside was a nest of large, white maggots.

Acne
See Zits

A chronic skin disease aggravated by poor hygiene which affects 80 per cent of adolescents, and for one per cent of the population can endure into middle age. The pores of the skin become blocked with sebum, the greasy secretion of the sebaceous glands, which then becomes infected with minute organisms that cause small lumps, or comerdones, mainly on the face, neck, back and chest. The eruption consists of little black spots or hard pimples usually with a blackhead on the top and small yellow pustules surrounded by red inflammations.

On the chin and neck of males the condition is aggravated by the blocking of hair follicles of the beard, so that the root of the hair becomes the centre of active inflammation. Squeezing such blemishes often results in a stump of hair, encased in a waxy sheath and attached to the dead root, easing itself loose from its pus-filled cavity.

Although acne is a well-established cause of anguish and often acute depression, particularly among aspiring adolescents, certain females who are particularly partial to hirsute, sweaty men have been known to be sexually attracted by ripe acne in their partners, even to the extent of squeezing their pustules and blackheads.

In the 1950s, when Elvis Presley and Richard Burton came to fame in the United States, they caused a craze for false acne patches. Packets of these could be purchased in drug stores for less than a dollar and consisted of small tinted rubber or plastic adhesions in various shades ranging from pink and yellow to a furious, bruised red, to be applied cosmetically to the naked flesh.

Different types were available, some young men preferring to emulate Presley's raw back and shoulders – much in demand among teenagers around swimming pools – while others chose to imitate the cratered cheeks and neck of the young Richard Burton. Burton himself once told how in the early 1960s, a young actress at a Hollywood party kissed a pustule that had just reached fruition on his jaw and burst – the pustule, that is, not the actress.

Amputation

Severing any limb or part of limb from the body. Over 5,000 amputations per year are carried out in Britain – mostly of the legs. More than 500 of these are double-leg amputations.

Modern surgical techniques are more sophisticated but, in the past, the victim was tied down and rum was poured down his throat. The rum bottle was also used to stun him when the pain became unbearable. After the amputation, even when the patient was not unconscious through shock or pain, the amputated stump was plunged into either a boiling vinegar solution or a vat of hot tar, as was usual on board ship after – or even during – naval battles.

Nelson's severed arm was cauterized in this way during the Battle of the Nile, and the excruciating pain was not restricted to the actual amputation, but used to revisit him at irregular and sometimes highly embarrassing moments. Once, at the height of a society ball in London, he was about to be introduced to the Prince Regent, when a scalding rush of pain contracted his severed stump under his coat, and he let out a howl like a wounded animal and fell ashen to the marble floor where he lay writhing.

Anal Retention

Literally, reluctance to part with the faeces causing severe constipation. Psychologically, this retentiveness can extend to fear of parting with a wide range of other substances and objects.

Perhaps the most famous sufferer from anal retention was the multi-millionaire Howard Hughes whose last words – as he died in his private plane – were 'insurance policy'.

Hughes could not bear his fingernails or toenails to be cut, so they grew until they curled up and he could neither walk nor use his hands. His hair was two feet long. He suffered from chronic constipation and when unable to prevent his bladder from emptying, kept his urine in jars which were stored in a closet.

Bacteria

These micro-organisms are the cause of many different diseases and are ubiquitous. Given the right conditions, general dampness and warmth, they multiply to an alarming degree. A bacillus can divide every thirty minutes so within 24 hours it would be possible for a single bacillus to generate 300,000,000,000 of its kind.

Bacteria are usually connected with disease but how many of us realise that a perfectly healthy human is the unwitting host of *more bacteria than there are people living on this planet*? These parasites are so minute that they could be crammed into a jam jar.

Bed Bugs

Tiny, blood-sucking parasites on humans. Wingless, flat and rusty-brown, bed bugs measure up to 5mm in length and 3mm wide. Their average life span is three to six months but they have the bizarre quality of being able to live for up to a year in a dormant state without food or water.

During the day, the bed bug lies hidden in cracks in walls, under loose wallpaper, or between floorboards but it is particularly happy in beds. Although it does not carry or transmit any known disease, the bed bug gives off a peculiarly foul aromatic smell, and its bites

leave a trail of irritating red spots. One of the authors discovered, in an exclusive French ski-ing resort, that her bed was infested with the creatures whose bites were impossible to scratch under layers of ski clothes. A few of the bugs managed to hitch-hike back to London and it was some weeks before they were finally eradicated.

The most effective antidote is a solution of DDT mixed with kerosene but more casual habitues of the bed bug domain may prefer to use lumps of slimy soap to stamp on the creatures and collect them up like blotting paper. No edible use has yet been found for the bed bug, unlike the cockroach (*qv*) instructions for peeling which – prior to consumption – are issued to the SAS.

In the seventeenth century, Charles II employed a personal 'Bug Destroyer to His Majestie' whose instructions were: 'Take gunpowder, lay it about the crevices in the bedstead, light it and keep the smoke in' and so he 'cured sixteen thousand beds of bugs, to great applause.'

Bed-Wetting

Bed-wetting is comparatively rare between early childhood and senility. When it does occur it is usually due to an excess of alcohol. The Creative Director of a successful London advertising agency was motoring

through France a few years ago when his car broke down in the mountains south of Grenoble. It was at the height of the summer holiday season and he and his companion found no room in any of the main hotels in the area. Eventually, they found a vacancy at a tiny dilapidated establishment owned by North Africans. After depositing their luggage they went out to dinner during which the Creative Director drank hugely. On returning to the hotel he passed out. During the night his companion was awakened by a sound like a running tap – but there was no tap or basin in the room. The sound continued for a long time and then slowly trickled to a halt. In the morning the Creative Director found himself lying on a sodden mattress beneath which the floorboards were soaked. The contents of his bladder had, it turned out, penetrated the plaster of the ceiling below and caused several hundred pounds' worth of damage.

The Creative Director hurriedly paid his bill and left the hotel, only to find that his car had not yet been repaired. He and his companion had to spend a further two days skulking in grimy lodgings in another part of the town, trying to avoid the wrath of the hotel's owners.

Bestiality

Strictly speaking, sexual intercourse with an animal, i.e. a non-human creature. The word bestiality has

been known to cause legal difficulties. In the 1930s a celebrated Irish barrister defended a man accused of buggering a duck. 'My client,' he told the court, 'is accused of bestiality with a duck. My Lord and Gentlemen and Ladies of the Jury, I respectfully submit that a duck is not, God forbid, a beast. It is a fowl.' His client was acquitted.

In 1952 a Nigerian resident of Paddington was arrested and committed for sexual indecency against a pigeon in Hyde Park. The charge of bestiality was eventually dropped, after Counsel had quoted from the aforementioned Irish case. The man was instead fined £10 for taking the pigeon home and eating it.

A more romantic example of bestiality is described by the celebrated war correspondent of the *Daily Express*, Sefton Delmer, in his vivid memoirs *Trail Sinister*. Here, Delmer recounts in a thinly disguised portrait the last amorous exploit of Philip Murray, a glamorous wayward socialite son of the great classical scholar and Oxford don Gilbert Murray. In the final days of the Spanish Civil War, young Murray *fils* found himself in the beleaguered town of Valencia, then still under Republican rule. Murray had been on an extended binge and was reduced, in Delmer's picturesque phrase, to a state of 'phobic moodiness and mad romantic exaltation in which love, hunger for love, threw him into delusions and despair.'

One evening, down in the squalid port area of Valencia, he met up at a street circus with a ferocious anarchist group calling themselves 'The Iron Guard of Karl Marx'. During the show, Murray's attention was drawn to a female chimpanzee – the circus's top attraction – 'a fine buxom she-ape with all the indications of her sex emphatically developed.'

Filled with misguided love, Murray tried to buy the

creature, offering a huge rate on the black market. When the circus owner rejected his offer, the Iron Guard of KM intervened; they called the owner a miserable, skulking capitalist – 'You refuse to part with this ape who is obviously dying with passion for the British compagnero!' – threatening to shoot him and burn down his circus if he did not agree.

Delmer then recounts how Murray and the ape, arm in arm with the Iron Guard of HM, proceeded on an extended tour of the town's bars and bodegas, during which the chimpanzee drank Fundador brandy glass for glass with her new admirer.

Finally, when they reached the plush Victoria Hotel, – the grandest in town and the HQ of the foreign press corps – the night porter refused them entry with the pompous words 'No apes allowed in the hotel.' The leader of the Iron Guard of KM, brandishing a pistol, shouted 'If you do not immediately permit the senora ape to enter the hotel with the Ingles, then we shall destroy the hotel and when we have finished there will be nothing left of the hotel or you.'

Murray and his ape duly repaired to his room, where he was last seen turning on the bath-water, and heard saying, as he closed the door, 'And now, my poppet, you shall have a lovely warm bath with plenty of lovely lavender soap. Do you like soap, oh Queen of my heart?'

Nothing was seen or heard of them for another 48 hours. The hotel personnel did not enter the room, partly because Murray had locked the door, but also because they were afraid – not only of the ape but of her peculiar English friend.

When a leading correspondent of the *Daily Mail*, William Forrest – who confirmed this story later to one of the authors – finally gained access to the room, he was greeted by a scene of unutterable chaos and squalor. The ape lay in a corner, huddled in a nest of pillows and blankets, and coughing horribly. Philip Murray lay in another corner, flushed with a high temperature and obviously very ill.

The British consul made arrangements for Murray, by this time almost delirious, to be evacuated to a British hospital ship, the Maine, lying off the coast at Alicante. But before this could take place, during his last moments of semi-lucidity, Murray – ever romantic – was able to despatch three cables to London – addressed to the three most eligible Society beauties, proposing marriage to each of them.

Murray died in the ambulance before reaching Alicante. The next morning – Delmer records – three telegrams arrived for Murray at the Victoria Hotel. They were from the girls to whom he had proposed. Two accepted him.

Delmer adds the foot note that a British doctor remarked afterwards that he had never seen a case of pneumonia like it, since this was a strain known only among apes, and he could not understand how a human had contracted it. Delmer and his colleagues kept faith with their dead companion and said nothing.

Body Ash

Dead skin cells are constantly shed from the body, especially at night when it rubs against the mattress leaving a trail of 'unnamed greasy particles, a de-hydrated version of what you get when you unblock the kitchen sink' as succinctly described by Sue

Arnold in the *Observer*. A salesman trying to sell her an extra powerful vacuum cleaner to rid her mattress of this 'body ash' said persuasively that 'Every year we get rid of a pound of rotten decaying stinking flesh and enough sweat to fill a bath, which goes straight into the mattress'.

All the cells in the body are replaced every seven years, which explains the ageing process, since the 'template' of genes which, as it were, designs the cells gradually becomes worn.

Botulism

Botulism is luckily a rare form of food poisoning. The victim's eye muscles stop focusing so vision becomes blurred. The eyelids droop and it is hard to speak. Next, swallowing becomes difficult and eventually the victim cannot even swallow his own saliva. Eventually, the chest muscles fail, breathing stops and the patient dies. Worst of all, his brain is clear throughout so he is aware of every stage of the agony.

Eight men decided to go fishing on Scotland's Loch Maree in 1923, taking duck-paste sandwiches for their lunch. Within a week, they were all dead, even though the duck paste had been made in a well-known food factory. However, the jars had not been heated to a high enough temperature after the paste had been put into them.

Food preserved at home is no safer. In America and Canada, many cases of botulism are caused by home-preserving string beans. Botulism is also a hazard of a North American Indian delicacy. A tribe on the Pacific coast makes 'salmon-egg cheese' which involves fermenting salmon eggs for several weeks, an ideal breeding ground for *Clostridium botulinum*. No doubt the resulting 'cheese' tastes delicious but death is all too often the result of eating it.

A few years ago, four old-age pensioners sat down to enjoy tinned salmon and salad for their evening meal. The tin – produced by a leading manufacturer – had a tiny hole in it which had allowed bacteria to enter. Almost immediately, the four old people were in agony; their throats swelled so that they could not swallow or breathe without pain. They were rushed to hospital where they underwent tracheotomy operations (a hole being cut directly into the wind-pipe) but soon afterwards they all died and sales of tinned salmon slumped.

Budgerigar Casserole

Budgerigars are popular throughout the world as pets giving enjoyment to young and old; their ability to learn to speak is well known. A less familiar attribute, however, is the flavour of their flesh. In London, a popular hostess serves budgerigar casserole to her guests who include the titled, rich and famous.

The recipe is a well-kept secret but the ingredients are said to include two budgerigars per person, gently simmered with herbs and vegetables. The bones, like those of sardines, are eaten with the flesh. Budgerigars are best consumed when young, and those used for breeding are spared from the pot – perhaps they might prove a little too muscular.

An added bonus of feeding budgerigars to one's guests is that their brightly coloured feathers can be used as table decorations, saving expense not only on meat but on flowers as well.

Budgerigar-fanciers Lung –
see Zoonoses

Burial

There are traditionally only three methods of disposing of dead bodies: burial, embalming (*qv*) and cremation. Burial is the earliest, most primitive and certainly the most disgusting, and owes its origins to the ancient Jewish religion and to the idea of the resurrection of the body, which has since passed into Christianity. For details of what happens after burial, see 'decomposition'.

The actual details apart, the practice of burying the

dead in consecrated ground – in churchyards within city limits – led to complications especially in the early part of the nineteenth century, when over-crowded churchyards full of cheap coffins bursting their contents turned such consecrated ground into a crawling abscess of putrefaction, distinguished by the rich, verdant flora which grew on the surface. But woe to any child which cut itself while playing in such surroundings, for gangrene frequently resulted. As a result, in the 1840s a number of laws were passed to curb the insanitary state of English churchyards, ordering that henceforth all cemeteries should be situated outside towns and cities.

Outside Europe and America, burial takes some strange forms. In the Malagash Republic, the dead are buried in brick kilns. After a year, with great ceremony, the stinking body is exhumed and reburied after a three-day festival accompanied by copious drinking of strong local brews, which help to deflect the smell. The Tukano Indians of South America, on the other hand, simply bury their dead under the earth floor of the family house or *maloca*. The corpse lies in a foetal position, its knees bound to its chest, and is placed in a burial vault lined with leaves. The hole is filled in and the family immediately resumes normal life.

The cost of a decent burial is inordinately high. Cheap burials, on the other hand, have their own grisly drawbacks. A notorious case was related to one of the authors by an expatriate Australian living in Tangier who made it his business to look after the interests of passing British visitors. In the late 1950s a young couple from Manchester arrived in the city for their honeymoon; being short of funds, they stayed at a cheap hotel and, while the young bride was taking her morning bath, a faulty electric fan fell into the water and electrocuted her. Distraught, the husband sought help from the Australian who advised him on the costs of local Moroccan funerals: the first, French-style, was far too expensive; the second, a simple Moslem internment, was more reasonable but he advised a third-class funeral.

Due to the heat, once the decision was taken the procedure was rapid. Later that afternoon, while he was comforting the young man over stiff drinks in Dean's Bar, a sleazy haunt of expatriate deviants in North Africa, they were disturbed by the sound of howling and wailing from outside. It was a quartet of professional mourners, all beggars covered in sores, who were following a mule on which was strapped a cardboard coffin. The end was open and out of it jutted the naked feet of the young Manchester bride on which flies were already settling.

Both the British Consul in Tangier, and later the British Ambassador in Rabat, made personal complaints to the Australian about what they considered 'disgusting conduct' from a Commonwealth citizen to a British subject. However, the bereaved husband held no resentment and ended up cohabiting with the Australian.

Austrians, on the other hand, are encouraged to donate their bodies to science with the promise of a funeral at the State's expense. All parts of the body, when dissected, are neatly labelled and are later reassembled like a jigsaw puzzle when ready for burial.

However, when King Philip the Handsome of Spain died suddenly in 1506 after a day of drinking, dancing and over-eating, his widow refused to let his body be buried at all and kept his decomposing body with her for three years; it shared her bed and accompanied her when travelling, to the extreme inconvenience of her subjects.

Cannibalism

The consumption of human flesh by another human is now rare and, with the exception of such notorious instances as the survivors of the Andes 'plane crash (as recounted in Piers Paul Read's book *Alive*) is usually to be found only in war time. There were, for example, a number of instances of cannibalism among American soldiers eating Japanese prisoners during the liberation of the Pacific Islands in World War II. The American slang for human flesh, in this context, is 'long pig' – believed to have originated because in texture and taste it is rich and very sweet, like pork.

There were also numerous instances of cannibalism in Russia after the Nazi invasion, notably in Leningrad during the 900-day siege. It became so prevalent that the Soviet authorities punished offenders with summary trial and execution – even leading, in several notorious cases, to the victims being themselves carved up and sold on the black market.

Perhaps the most famous incident of cannibalism in British legal history is the so-called 'Cabin Boy Case' in the 1890s. The survivors of a shipwreck were eventually picked up after being at sea for several weeks in a lifeboat, with only limited supplies of food and drinking water. At the time, they were considered lucky to be alive; but later, following their drunken boasting after they reached port, ugly rumours began to circulate that they cheated death only by eating the cabin boy whom they had listed as 'missing, believed drowned'.

Eventually, the police took them in for questioning. They broke down, confessed, and were charged with murder. A sensational trial ensued which ended with each of them being sentenced to only nine months' imprisonment. This led to a remark by a High Court judge at the time who said: 'Damn funny country we live in. Kill a cabin boy and eat him and you get nine months. Bugger him and you get two years.'

There are also rare cases of unintentional cannibalism. One of the authors, while up at Cambridge during the 1950s, recalls the evening when Dr Jonathan Miller – then a medical student – was dining in a local Indian restaurant and found an unusual bone in his chicken curry. It so happened that he had been studying the anatomy of the human hand that day, and the bone's shape and size were strikingly familiar. Going into the kitchens, Miller saw that one of the cooks had a heavily bandaged hand; his little finger was missing.

Cannibalism has also intruded into the field of politics. In the mid-Fifties in the French Camerouns, a local politician – Victor Biakaboda – was eaten by his constituents while canvassing in the last General Election before the country became independent. This led to a major political crisis, since the Colonial administration refused to hold a bye-election in the absence of a death certificate but none could be issued because there was no body.

Castration

The removal of penis and/or testicles, usually by force but occasionally self-inflicted. Castration has in the past been used as a punishment (see Masturbation); in the late eighteenth century one James Trotter was castrated because he had sired three illegitimate children whose up-bringing had to be paid for by his local Parish Council. The operation was carried out by the pig butcher.

Self-mutilation often has a religious basis. An example of this, taken quite literally to its logical extreme, was recorded some three years ago in the *Daily Telegraph* and concerned a couple living in a small Oxfordshire town. During a prayer session at home, the husband suddenly produced a cut-throat razor and, in front of his wife, pulled down his trousers, cut off his penis and threw it on the fire (see also Self-immolation). Neither history nor the admirable *Daily Telegraph* recounts the fate of this gentleman, except that he was rushed to hospital with severe blood loss and his life was saved.

Origines Adamantius, known as Origen, who was born in Egypt in the second century AD became famous as a Christian philosopher. Not only did he castrate himself in the pursuit of religious zeal but many others followed his example.

Some fifteen centuries earlier, another Egyptian showed a propensity for castration though not, this

31

time, self-inflicted. King Menephta achieved a remarkable score which is recorded on a monument at Karnak. In battle, he cut off his enemies' penises and brought home a total of 13,240 – nearly half of which were forcibly removed from Libyans.

Castration was not always forcible or self-inflicted. Eunuchs, often deliberately castrated as children in order to qualify later for influential positions at court, were found in civilisations as far apart as ancient Egypt and Imperial China whose last Emperor ruled until 1911. In China, eunuchs desiring to enter the Imperial service had to present their dismembered organs, pickled in a jar, as proof of their suitability. In 1920, a Western journalist chanced upon a home for former eunuchs of the Imperial Court. Most had been totally castrated – penis and testicles removed – which caused a weak bladder and obliged them to urinate through a quill.

As recently as 1890, boy sopranos were castrated to prevent their voices from breaking. These 'castrati' played a vital part both in ecclesiastical music and in opera, particularly in eighteenth-century Italy, which may have gone some way towards redeeming the loss of their own vital parts.

Catheter (urethral)

A gruesome instrument used for investigations of the bladder or prostate gland. The catheter slides up the nozzle of the penis, usually while the patient is fully conscious and aware – a practice much favoured by French doctors. Catheters may be made of plastic, rubber, silver or glass; they are usually straight but are sometimes bent. Some have an eye near the tip, or a whistle-shaped end with an open tip which is used when there is a risk of the catheter running into obstructions such as large clots of blood. Others have a small balloon at the end which, when inflated, keeps the instrument steady and stops it from slipping out.

Certain male homosexuals are said to derive pleasure from the application of this instrument. A New York night club, The Mineshaft, which specialises in such arcane pleasures recently exhibited a photograph on the wall of its lobby depicting a double catheter being inserted into a penis.

Caul

Originally the word for a hair-net worn by women. It was later used to describe the silken, almost transparent skin or membrane enclosing the intestines. Thus, God instructed Moses: 'Thou shalt take all the fat that covereth the innards and the caul that is above the liver.' Its present-day meaning, though, describes the membraneous bag within the womb which contains the waters during pregnancy and which sometimes covers a child when it is born.

In the eighteenth and nineteenth centuries it was widely regarded as a lucky charm, and many families kept them as heirlooms.

The *Morning Post* carried this advertisement in 1815:

A child's caul to be disposed of, particularly recommended to persons going to the Continent on pleasure or business, officers in his Majesty's navy, merchants trading to the East and West Indies, and all other parts of the globe, being exposed to the dangers of the seas, having the caul in their possession their life will most assuredly always be preserved.

However, Byron was born with a caul over his head as well as with a club foot and always regarded the caul as a curse.

Chagas' Disease

Widespread in Central and South America, Chagas' Disease is carried by tiny insects known as 'barber beetles' which inhabit cracks in the walls of houses. The only way of controlling the disease – for which there is no cure – is through exterminating the barber beetles. This is almost impossible unless the house is kept spotlessly clean, so the masses of poverty-stricken people living in shanty towns are extremely susceptible while the rich are less often affected.

Chagas' Disease causes the irrevocable deterioration of the heart and the victim suffers increasing weakness which can last for years before his inevitable death. A leading Brazilian publisher recently told one of the authors that he was asked, at a chic dinner party in Rio, what is the difference between Chagas' Disease and AIDS. He replied: 'You get Chagas' Disease from barbers and AIDS from hairdressers'.

Cheese

Bacteria and mould play a vital role in the making of cheese. 'Blue' cheeses such as Stilton and Roquefort are injected with certain bacteria to achieve their distinctive veins. The 'bloom' on cheeses such as Brie and Camembert is a type of mould which is sprayed on. Another vital ingredient is rennet, an enzyme taken from the fourth stomach of a freshly-killed calf. Hardly surprising, then, that the Chinese regard cheese as nauseating although it is eaten in various forms and flavours by almost every other nation.

Sometimes, extraordinary steps are taken to improve the flavour of cheese. In 1888, J.G. Bourke (author of *Scatalogical Rites of All Nations*) received a letter from one Dr Gustav Jaeger. He wrote that:

A storekeeper in Berlin was punished some years ago for having used the urine of young girls with a view to make his cheese richer and more piquant.

Notwithstanding, people went, bought and ate his cheese with delight.

Chyme

Partly digested food, highly acidic and greyish, as it passes in a semi-liquid mass from the stomach into the intestine. One of the authors has some evidence that the food increases in volume as it is transformed into chyme. The late Julian Jebb, grandson of Hilaire Belloc, was once dining in a smart Chelsea restaurant with the Managing Director of a small London publishing company specialising in belles lettres. The latter had had too much to drink, and after consuming a plate of *spaghetti alla carbonara*, suddenly began to regurgitate it slowly almost fastidiously, on to the plate from which he had recently eaten.

Jebb watched, in fascinated horror, as the plate filled and then over-flowed on to the table, noticing that far more food seemed to issue from the stomach of his friend than had entered it.

Circumcision

If it were discovered today that a primitive tribe was mutilating the genital organs of its new-born males, or that such atrocities were being carried out in secret laboratory experiments on animals, there would be an outcry among rights campaigners of every description (except, perhaps, militant feminists who would probably campaign for all male organs to be removed completely at birth).

However, this operation is carried out everywhere in the 'civilised' world, not solely because of medical necessity or even for religious reasons. Although circumcision is no longer as fashionable as formerly, over four thousand Americans are circumcised every day and, of these, more than seventy thousand per year suffer 'excessive penile loss'.

Among ethnic minorities, female circumcision is also common. The clitoris is removed, often without anaesthetic. This practice was also used as recently as the nineteenth century in America, Britain and Europe to prevent female masturbation (*qv*). White-hot irons were applied to the clitoris or silver wire sutures were used to pierce and cover it. Similar treatment was given to male masturbators though perhaps the most severe punishment took place in Texas in the 1890s: the complete amputation of a penis (see Castration).

Cockroaches

Crawling all too near the surface of the glossy, upwardly mobile lives of millions of city dwellers are even more millions of cockroaches. These hardy creatures adore the trappings of twentieth-century civilisation, preferring damp, warm places though they have been known to inhabit the hinges of refrigerator doors. One woman, trying to find out why her bedside alarm clock had stopped, discovered a nest of cockroaches happily living in its works.

There are over three thousand kinds of cockroaches though there are three main species which join top London gentlemen's clubs and are particularly partial to expensive restaurants. In New York, the most prevalent variety is called 'the small German', followed by 'the big brown American' and 'the big black Oriental'.

Cockroaches are equally happy at sea. Beverley Cross, in his excellent book *Mars in Capricorn*, remembers:

> I found the coffee-grinder black with cockroaches – it was hard to tell coffee-bean from insect, and I fear the resulting powder was an equal share, but there were no complaints. Cockroaches were everywhere in the ship but one soon became used to them. The first time I picked up a loaf I carefully cut off the end piece, which was crawling with them, and took the next slice. Within two days however, I was as hardened as anyone else and scarcely bothered to brush them off the bread before eating it.

The Russian-born artist, Chaim Soutine, lived in great luxury at the Ritz Hotel in Paris in the Twenties but never washed or changed his clothes. A doctor, examining him because of ear-ache, discovered the cause: a nest of cockroaches living in the artist's ear.

Cockroaches can survive for up to two weeks without water and three weeks without food. Nothing daunts them, not even poison – to which they can build up an immunity – or lack of their favourite diet of human food. Cockroaches infesting hospitals have been known to eat nothing but used surgical swabs for as long as ten weeks. They are also partial to eating human faeces – and each other. Since they can crawl through a crack thinner than a penny, flattening their hard-shelled, shiny bodies, it is almost impossible to keep them under control.

The British Pest Control Association recently announced that almost all hospitals are infested with cockroaches and other disease-bearing insects. A Welsh environmental health officer whose wife is a night-nurse at a local hospital killed sixteen adult cockroaches on her ward, and many more in the kitchen, during a single visit. The *Daily Mirror* reported cockroaches served up in a chicken stew to patients at the Royal Free Hospital, London, in 1985.

One of the authors, staying at a large country house in Gloucestershire, felt hungry during the night and went to the kitchen. The pattern on the linoleum seemed unusually dark and she realised that the floor was covered with cockroaches. Some had climbed on to the kitchen table and were consuming the remains of a cheese souffle with the help of several mice, while a bat circled overhead. She retreated, shrieking, to be asked coldly by her host what all the fuss was about. Clearly, country gentlemen are used to having their homes invaded by all forms of wild life.

In fact, had the mice not preferred the souffle, they

might well have fallen on the cockroaches since rats and mice eat them 'like popcorn' according to *New York Magazine*. Lizards love eating them too – but giving these predators free rein in our homes could cause other problems.

One solution could be to promote the cockroach as a gourmet delicacy; they are already popular in what pass for smart restaurants in Jakarta, capital of Indonesia, and are certainly cheaper than caviar.

Contraception

The various contraceptives now available are considerably less disgusting than earlier methods. The ancient Egyptians inserted crocodile dung into the vagina; elephant's dung was also used. In ancient Rome, a goat's bladder was placed in the vagina which seems simpler than the alternative method of removing two worms from a spider's body and wrapping them in animal hide which was then fixed to the woman's body. This – according to Pliny – was the best way to prevent conception.

More recently, though in the pre-Pill days of the 1950s, pessaries were popular with those who disliked tiresome condoms. These came in various patented forms: some jelly-like, others like shaving foam which stung both penis and vagina, and a variety resembling brown toffees. These were known as 'Rendall's – The Wife's Best Friend' (a wedding ring had to be worn for their purchase) and had an unfortunate drawback: large, brown concentric circles stained the undersheet after use.

A successful Fleet Street journalist (now, alas, dead) was already very ambitious when at Cambridge and was keen to be well respected in College. One afternoon, a friend of his 'borrowed' his room in order to seduce (without much difficulty) a blue-stocking girl from Girton, having procured some Rendall's in advance. Inevitably, traces of their ardour remained. The 'bedder' (cleaning woman) was later overheard saying: 'The dirty man's gone and done his business in the bed'. Years later, the friend mentioned the incident to the journalist who turned on him in fury: 'So that's why my bedder was so cool towards me during my last term! I hope to goodness she didn't tell the Provost!'

Also in the 1950s, one of the authors was invited to stay at a villa in Spain with his girl-friend's family. She preferred to use a contraceptive jelly which was sold in jars and had both the appearance and the consistency of rough paté de campagne. The lid carried the instruction 'Keep Cool' so she put the jar in the refrigerator.

One morning, the young couple were startled to find the girl's father – a humourless oil company executive – spreading their contraceptive jelly on toast. Too embarrassed to explain its true nature, they watched him eat it in silence. There were no apparently adverse effects.

Copraphilia

A noisome habit and extreme sexual perversion involving the eating of human excrement. Psychologists are divided as to the cause of this peculiar taste but it is generally believed to be associated with deep-seated anxieties about bodily functions which have their origins far back in childhood, and to be associated with unhappy and often coercive methods of potty-training.

In the 1970s it was common on New York's fashionable East Side to find certain upwardly mobile couples, both heterosexual and homosexual, keeping portions of their partner's excrement in the refrigerator, often tastefully disguised in small jars which had previously contained caviar or foie gras.

A particularly graphic case of copraphilia came to the notice of one of the authors in the summer of 1948 while he was at prep school in Sussex. The mother of one of his fellow pupils was an exotic and much-married socialite, at the time attached to one of the richest industrialists of the day. During the school's sports weekend, she and her husband had booked into a smart hotel nearby. After their first night there, however, they were abruptly asked to leave – no reasons given but obviously under a cloud – with instructions never to return. The author discovered the reason from an impeccable source, someone who had known the industrialist's first wife.

This earlier marriage, contracted before the Second World War, had been curtailed after only a week of what had been planned as a three-month honeymoon cruise on the industrialist's private yacht, and was followed by an immediate divorce. He had apparently asked his wife if he could consume a portion of her excrement for breakfast every morning. One can only conclude that the Sussex hotel – despite being enormously flattered to have such rich and famous guests – was obviously not prepared to cater to their every whim.

Nor is copraphilia solely restricted to sexual tastes. At Cambridge University in the early Fifties, a notoriously rich and dissolute undergraduate had a habit of taunting less fortunate members of his College. On one occasion – he offered a very poor young man the sum of £500 (an enormous amount in those days) to eat a plate of faeces. It is recorded that the undergraduate, after getting suitably drunk, agreed. However, he had consumed only a couple of mouthfuls when he discovered a hair on his plate and was sick.

(See also Fartleberries)

Cosmetic Surgery

One of the authors, waiting for the curtain to rise in a Broadway theatre, overheard the woman sitting behind her ask a friend: 'What did Sadie get for her eighteenth birthday the fur coat or the nose job?'

Some fifty-five thousand 'nose jobs' are carried out each year in the United States where one can often spot a lady with a perfect nose that unfortunately doesn't match the rest of her face. A similar number of operations are carried out to remove bags from under the eyes, while over 350,000 people under-go a full face lift. (see also Legs, length of)

Another popular operation is breast enlargement which is performed on 200 American women per day. The same techniques are used for trans-sexuals (*qv*). An unfortunate side-effect can occur if the injected silicone slips out of place causing unexpected bulges in places as far distant from the breasts as the ankles. Breast reduction is less popular; it involves removing a section of flesh from each breast, the nipples then being stitched back into place on the re-shaped breast. Other women simply have their breasts lifted. Cosmetic Surgery is not, however, popular in Papua New Guinea where it is common to see topless native women with one huge breast hanging down to the waist while the other retains a more normal shape. The authors have been unable to discover an explanation for this phenomenon.

Perhaps the most famous recent case of unsuccessful cosmetic surgery was the woman who sued her surgeon because, in lifting her stomach, he had moved her navel two inches to the left causing her embarrassment when she wanted to wear a bikini.

However, this art (or science) has been practised for many years. One of the first cases, shortly after World War I, was the late Peggy Guggenheim who had a somewhat overlarge nose. At enormous expense, she offered herself as an early guinea-pig in cosmetic surgery. The operation was not a success. Within days of the bandages being removed, her nose swelled to the size, shape and texture of a rather old potato.

Another unfortunate case involved a famous Society beauty, Gladys, Duchess of Marlborough, who felt that her much-admired nose wasn't quite perfect and underwent surgery shortly before her marriage.

The sockets of her enormous eyes were becoming puffed and distorted as the wax melted beneath the flesh and entered the intricate orifices surrounding her high cheekbones. Two brownish channels gradually appeared to the right and left of her nose, terminating each side of her chin in small horn-like protruberances.

(From *The Face on the Sphinx* by Daphne Fielding

The marriage did not last and all trace of Gladys was obliterated from Blenheim Palace but for a carved replica of her lost beauty on a stone sphinx.

Creeping Eruption

A species of roundworm (*qv*), *Strongyloides stercoralis*, prevalent in the tropics produces larvae which burrow under the skin leaving a long 'creeping' red trail. Apart from the appalling itching this produces, the larvae also cause severe diarrhoea (*qv*).

Crucifixion

Crucifixion is a myth so embodied in Christianity that the details are almost entirely glossed over or ignored. Until AD 337 when it was abolished by the first Christian Emperor of Rome, Constantine the Great, it was the established method of execution throughout the civilised world and was used as a punishment for offences and crimes which today would rate only a moderately stiff fine or short custodial sentence.

Such executions were carried out *en masse*. The Coliseum in Rome was often bristling with crosses and full of the horrible screams of the dying. After the defeat of the Spartacus uprising in BC 71, over six thousand crosses lined the Appian Way into Rome, each bearing a gladiator or slave.

It was a truly atrocious method of death, and various refinements made it more so. The cross used for Christ's execution – and for most others at the height of the Roman Empire – was not, in fact, a cross but a low wooden frame in the shape of a T, without a headpiece. The cross-piece or 'patibulum' was made of heavy cypress wood and weighed over 100 lb. It was this which Christ had to carry the seven hundred yards from Pilate's Praetorium to Golgotha.

The square nails were not driven through the hands, which would have torn under the weight of the body, but between the main wrist-bones. This had the effect not only of tearing the flesh but of causing the same pain as an intense and prolonged sprained wrist. The pain was further increased by the median nerve which crosses the wrist joint and was usually distended over the square-edged nails without being cut through. This caused cramp in both hands so that, as the nail went in, the thumb was bent violently across the palm and the thumb-nail dug deeply into the flesh.

When the victim was splayed out across the patibulum, he could be hoisted up so that the cross-beam could be slotted on to the vertical post or '*stipes*'. As soon as this was done, the knees were bent up until the sole of one foot was pressed flat against the *stipes*, and another eight-inch nail was driven through it, exactly between the second and third metatarsal bones. Once the point of the nail came through the sole of the foot, the second leg was pressed into position so that the same nail could be hammered through the outer foot and then into the wooden post.

The body was then left to hang, its whole weight suspended from three nails. Loss of blood is said to have been slight but the pain would have been insufferable and the death agony would have begun almost at once.

The weight of the body sagging downwards would produce a terrible tension in the arms and shoulders, and – most damagingly – in the chest wall where the ribs were pulled upwards so that the whole rib-cage became permanently distended as though the victim had just taken in an enormously deep breath – but could not breathe out. The victim began to suffocate from the weight of his own body.

At the same time, cramps began in the arm, shoulder and chest muscles which were starved of oxygen. As a result, too much lactic acid entered the bloodstream – a complaint often suffered by athletes. These excruciating cramps combined with the near-impossibility of breathing so that the body became poisoned with carbon dioxide and death followed through suffocation. In lucky cases, this would occur in less than half an hour.

However, the Romans would vary this time-scale according to whim or judgement. Death could be prolonged by using ropes instead of nails to sustain the hands, or by fixing a narrow seat to the vertical post, or a block under the sole of the feet. By these means the death throes could be made to last between three to five hours. Death could also be hastened by breaking the legs, so that the victim could not thrust himself upwards and gain more leverage for breathing.

A detailed medical diagnosis of Christ's death has been recounted by Professor Smallhout of University Hospital, Utrecht, Holland, who has charted Our Lord's death throes over six hours.

In modern times, religious fanatics – usually in South America or the Philippines – re-enact the Crucifixion before huge, bemused crowds. Death is usually swift, unless the local police have already been alerted and intervene. Some of these incidents, including some carried out in comparative privacy and not always with the full co-operation of the victim – have been filmed and illicitly sold as 'snuff movies'. At least one case in Mexico City and another in Manila are officially classed as unsolved murders.

Cryogenics

The science of freezing bodies after death and reviving them when a cure is found for the disease that killed them. The most famous reputed cryogenics 'guinea pig' is Walt Disney whose body is apparently kept frozen in a secret room in Sleeping Beauty's Palace in Disneyland. Others are said to include Einstein and Onassis.

Scientists in the Soviet Union have reportedly resuscitated six men frozen eight years ago after death from heart disease. However, their new lease of life may not prove enjoyable. 'They are no better off than they were just before being frozen, but no worse off either' according to a report in a Soviet medical journal.

Cysts

Hollow tumours which contain fluid or soft matter. These can be found in any part of the body but vary according to their location (see Ovarian cysts). Pet-lovers should beware of hyatid cysts, a common result of allowing dogs which carry tapeworm to contaminate food for human consumption. The larval tapeworm can cause cysts in the human liver which grow as large as a man's head if left untreated.

In the tropics there are many bizarre growths and cysts due to alien parasites, such as one which causes small hard discs like light-coloured scabs to appear on the skin. These eventually detach themselves from the surrounding skin and open like small flaps or manhole covers, revealing tiny heads of parsitic insects or blind, worm-like creatures.

Death, causes of

All of us must die sooner or later. Cancer and heart disease are the two major killers. Entering hospital is no guarantee that death will be staved off; in the United States nearly fifty thousand hospital patients die each year from 'inadequate nutritional care' quite apart from the 9,000 who die as a result of unnecessary operations.

How much more interesting death must have been in former times; the *Annual Register* for 1809 listed one death from 'overjoy' and five from 'grief'; 'bursten and rupture' accounted for fifteen, as did 'colick and gripes', while 'convulsions claimed no less than 3,463. Other causes of death that year included:-

Evil	2
Jaw Locked	4
St Anthony's Fire	2
Water in the Head	252
Worms	5

Decomposition

Changes that take place in plants and animals after death, causing their bodies to disintegrate into carbonic acid gas and ammonia. This is caused by bacteria and involves the production of a number of poisonous and foul substances: in the case of the human body, alkaloids known as 'putrescene' and 'cadaverene'. These give off a uniquely unpleasant smell which is difficult to describe, except that it is revoltingly sweet and cloying, and once experienced is never forgotten; nor does any amount of exposure to it lessen its overwhelming repellence.

In a temperate climate, and without refrigeration, decomposition – or putrefaction – in the human body sets in within forty-eight hours of death, although the first traces of the smell can be detected within twenty-four hours. In very hot, particularly humid climates the process is greatly accelerated, so that the corpse becomes repellent within only a few hours, and the smell and change of colour is usually accompanied by the whole body swelling up.

The first visible sign of putrefaction is a darkening of the skin over the lower part of the stomach or back, caused by the blood draining downwards. This is followed by a faint greenish-brown tinge which sets in within three days, if the corpse has not already been buried or refrigerated. Within two to three weeks the whole body is an amorphous dark, spongy brown and green, with blotches of dark red; the flesh begins to collapse, the skin to shrivel, and the features become almost unrecognisable. By the end of one year, the organs have disintegrated; within four to seven years bodies buried in open ground have been reduced to skeletons.

Bodies that have been left in water decompose more slowly, and in the early stages the process is particularly disgusting since the body swells up with gases within a couple of weeks. Such corpses, known in the police vernacular as 'floaters', are extremely disagreeable to handle, especially if they burst. The skin becomes white and waxen – a process known as 'saponification' – taking on the texture of soap; the body is broken down into fatty acids and poisonous, volatile substances called 'adipocere'. In some circumstances, this process may last for years – even in very deep water where there is little or no oxygen, for eternity.

One of the trickier moral problems of exploring the wreck of the 'Titanic' lying two and a half miles down in the freezing North Atlantic, is that any pictures of the interior of the ship or of the surrounding sea-bed could not help showing in detail some of the one thousand five-hundred-odd corpses which – according to expert medical evidence – would not have fully decomposed, even after more than seventy years.

A former Royal Navy diving expert, who now works as a salvage consultant, said: 'I have observed the condition of many bodies in wrecks, mostly from the Second World War and usually at a depth of two hundred feet. In those conditions you find the bones picked dry by the fish. Sometimes, in water-tight compartments or sealed bulkheads, you get bodies that have burst out of their uniforms and are like huge wax porpoises. They are truly nightmarish. The tongue pokes out of the mouth and the intestines literally explode out of the stomach and anus. The hands become like bunches of bananas. Pretty odd, I can tell you, next to all that gold braid!'

It is interesting to note that among the last organs

to disintegrate are the eyeballs which shrink and, eventually, melt into small jellied globules like raisins.

While all forms of putrefaction are affected by the temperature, humidity and conditions in which the body is buried, the process is also dependent – particularly in the early stages – on the contents of the stomach at the time of death, and on whether the body suffered mutilation.

One of the authors observed large numbers of dead bodies in the Sinai Desert in the aftermath of the Six Day War in June 1967. These had all been dead between nine and ten days, and all had suffered violent deaths. The smell, even without the wind, was detectable several miles away. Most of the bodies – almost all of young men – were blackened and in many cases dehydrated by the intense sun and dry desert air. But, in a few cases, they had swollen grotesquely, lying like balloons with arms and legs extended in the air.

In 1962, the same author was shown round a morgue in Oran, Algeria, during a strike by French undertakers. Ten European bodies lay unburied – one woman and nine men – all of whom had died violently, most of them with their throats cut. There was no refrigeration, and the only precaution taken was an irregular dowsing of the floors and tables with powerful disinfectant.

Most of them had been dead for ten days or two weeks; but one, placed in an open coffin, had lain unburied for six weeks. Looking inside, the author saw the coffin's contents, which can only be described as looking like a mixture of Camembert and spinach. Outside, French army defaulters were being made to clean up the place as a punishment. Before leaving, one of them took the author aside and showed him what looked like a pile of live whitebait which had been shovelled behind a hedge. These, he explained, were 'vers' – worms, or white maggots, each the size and shape of a fingernail. They had been extracted from the open wounds of the corpses in the morgue. When the author – then working as a foreign correspondent in Algeria – telephoned his London newspaper and described the scene, his Foreign Editor commented: 'Not quite family breakfast reading, old boy!'

Devonshire Colic

Sharp. spasmodic pains in the stomach caused by excess consumption of cider which has been stored in lead-lined containers. Renowned for giving rise to inordinately bombastic farts (*qv*).

Diarrhoea

Diarrhoea is a symptom of many digestive disorders and illnesses. This watery excrement, in extreme cases resembling a thin brown soup, is commonly the result of food poisoning. The consumption of under-cooked beans is a little-known cause of appalling diarrhoea accompanied by loud explosions of flatulence, all too prevalent among the haute bohemians of London's Islington and Holland Park.

However, embarrassment caused by diarrhoea is not confined to the digestive system. The late Tom Driberg (see Semen), Member of Parliament for Barking before his elevation to the house of Lords as Lord Bradwell, recorded in his ebullient memoirs, *Ruling Passions*, that among his many conquests was a young down-and-out:

> . . . still without speaking . . . he folled over with his back towards me, his bottom pressing against my genitals . . . The actual entry was, I fear, I must say, suspiciously easy: this meant either that the orifice had been coated with Vaseline (or the rather better-class 'K.Y.') to facilitate previous entries, or that my bed-mate was suffering from diarrhoea, a common by-product of dietary impoverishment. The latter, alas, proved to be the case, as a saffron smear on the cheap cotton sheet testified.

Doner Kebabs

A Public Health Inspector recently called on a doner kebab take-away restaurant in London's West End.

Being particularly diligent, he insisted on slicing through the huge revolving hunk of compressed layers of meat from which customers were currently being served. As he cut through to the centre, he found a soft core heaving with white maggots.

But, besides maggots, doner kebabs provide the ideal environment for salmonella bacteria. Revolving slowly on the spit, the centre of the meat never reaches a high enough temperature to kill off its parasites, but instead remains at a medium temperature highly conducive to their multiplication. Recent figures show that food poisoning is on the increase in Britain, a fact which cannot be unconnected with the recent rise in popularity of take-away food.

The origin of the meat used in doner kebabs is itself sometimes food for speculation. A few years ago there were potent rumours that doner kebab houses in Kilburn, North London, were serving portions of the missing Derby winner Shergar, kidnapped in Ireland in 1982.

Dysentery

There are two types of dysentery, bacillary and amoebic. Both are caused by eating contaminated food or by drinking infected water, especially if it has been polluted by the excrement of someone already suffering from the disease. The infection can also be spread by flies (*qv*) and by the unhygenic handling of food.

Dysentery causes severe and uncontrollable diarrhoea (*qv*) often tainted by blood, which is why it is also known as 'bloody flux', and can occur up to fifty times a day in acute cases. Especially in amoebic dysentery, the intestines (*qv*) may be perforated, and abscesses (*qv*) appear in the brain, testes, liver and bones.

A fifty per cent mortality rate used to be common, though both types of the disease are now controllable by drugs. In the ancient world, though, it was a common cause of death. When Tutankhamen's tomb was opened, encysted amoeba were discovered which had remained undisturbed for five thousand years and were still capable of causing amoebic dysentery.

Pliny recommended that 'camel's dung, reduced into ashes, and incorporat with oile, doth curle and frizzle the hair of the head, and taken in drinks, as much as a man may comprehend with three fingers, cureth the dysenterie.'

Ear Wax

Why the body produces this thick, yellow, clinging substance remains a mystery. Unpleasant to the touch and taste, wax can cause deafness if allowed to build up over the years into a plug but cleaning should be done with care and in privacy. There is a disturbing trend towards carrying out this occupation in public places with the finger-nail (see also Nose-picking).

No use has been found for ear wax (also known as 'cerumen') although Jan Ven Helmont recommended in 1662 that it was 'a great comfort in the pricking of the sinews'.

Embalming

Embalming aims to prevent, or at least postpone, the effects of decomposition (*qv*). The ancient Egyptians pioneered this process, removing the brain and entrails which were kept in specially-made pots. They rubbed down the body with palm wine, scattered it with purifying spices and wrapped it in bandages. However, it may well have been the dry desert air and cool conditions inside the pyramids which were actually responsible for the good state of preservation of mummified bodies.

In the United States, embalming is big business – brilliantly described in Jessica Mitford's classic book *The American Way of Death*. Unless a specific request is made not to embalm a body the mortician goes to work immediately. The blood is drained and replaced with three to six gallons of embalming fluid – usually a mixture of glycerine, formaldehyde, borax, phenol and alcohol, plus perfume to disguise the medicinal smell and dye (available in a variety of shades) to restore a healthy glow to the skin. The contents of the stomach and intestines are drawn out through a suction pump and replaced with 'cavity fluid'. As Jessica Mitford points out, few people die in the full bloom of health so running repairs are carried out: the lips are sewn together, often over a 'Natural Expression Former' and in a smiling position; swollen features are flattened, sunken ones plumped up with injections of massage cream. Make-up is applied (to men as well as women), hair is styled, hands manicured, and the body dressed (see Funeral Fashions). The deceased may be given a life-like prop such as a pipe or – especially in the case of literary and film agents – a telephone.

It is ironical that – because the less preservative used in the embalming fluid, the more life-like the deceased's body – the expensive good looks endowed by embalming may hardly last beyond the funeral. A Californian pathologist is quoted as saying that 'an exhumed embalmed body is a repugnant, mouldy, foul-looking object.' Only ten weeks after the burial, he saw a man 'covered with mould, long whiskers of penicillin'.

Modern attempts at permanent preservation are notoriously unsuccessful – as witnessed, typically, in the Soviet Union where in 1984 a startled British visitor to Lenin's tomb in Moscow saw the right ear drop off the remains of the architect of modern Communism. *Or were they Lenin's remains?* An authoritative source has since claimed that attempts to embalm Lenin's body after his death in 1924 were unsuccessful and that an understudy was substituted. However, in the rush to provide a new 'body', it was not noticed that Lenin Mark II possessed considerably more hair in death than the real Lenin had even as a young man.

Accidental embalming can be remarkably successful. In his book *The Bog People*, the late Professor P.V. Glob described how, in May 1950, two Danish farmers discovered a body in a peat bog, so perfectly preserved that it was at first thought to be the victim of a recent murder. It turned out that the man had been ritually sacrificed two thousand years earlier.

The most complete and enduring form of embalming is by deep freezing (see also Cryogenics). A recent newspaper report tells of a small girl opening the deep-freeze in search of ice-cream and finding her missing grandmother inside. In 1865, during the first successful ascent of the Matterhorn, four of Edward Whymper's team fell from the summit and plunged more than six thousand feet to the glacier below. Two of the bodies were never recovered; but they are due to reappear within the next five years, dressed in their Victorian Sunday best, wearing walking shoes, and still carrying the frayed clothes line whose fracture catapulted them to their death.

Excrement

More than six hundred tons of dog faeces are

deposited in Britain each day. 'Pooper-scoopers', already essential equipment for New York dog owners, may soon be introduced. In Paris, a specially-equipped team scours the city on motor-bikes and deposits the droppings of three-quarters of a million dogs into the Seine (no wonder the French drink so much bottled water) at a cost to the city of £2,000,000 per year.

A well-known London publisher some years ago slipped on a dog turd while waving goodbye to a friend, fracturing his thigh. This necessitated a long, painful and extremely costly stay in a private hospital, making it perhaps the most expensive dog turd in history.

Expressions involving excrement in the English language are lamentably restricted to what the admirable Eric Partridge calls 'low, colloquial, abusive'. The French, however, are altogether less mealy-mouthed. 'Chie-en-lit' – literally, one who shits in his bed – was a favourite expletive of Charles de Gaulle which he lavished publicly on such esteemed colleagues and compatriots as Marshal Petain, General Salan and Jacques Soustelle. Jean-Paul Sartre, however, had the distinction of being described as a 'chie-in-lit de premier cru'.

A vivid case of 'Chie-en-lit' in action concerned a distinguished English man of letters renowned for his chronicles of low life. Some years ago, he stayed with his fiancee at her parents' house en route for a motoring holiday on the Continent. Her mother, being somewhat old-fashioned, put them in separate rooms. The gentleman in question imbibed heavily during dinner (his future father-in-law had an excellent cellar). During the small hours, nature called – but not loudly enough. In his sleep he experienced an accident common among heavy drinkers – a 'liquid fart'.

In the confusion of their early departure next morning, he made no attempt to clean up the bed, but simply pulled up the covers and left without explanation to his future in-laws or his fiancee. The awful realisation of what he had done pursued him across France but, not wishing to disrupt the idyllic happiness of his companion, it was evening before he decided to broach the subject. Facing his beloved across the table he said: 'Darling, there's something I have to tell you.' She gazed deep into his eyes: 'You don't have to tell me, darling. You love me. And I love you too.' The marriage did not last long.

It is a commonly-held myth that burglars defecate in the homes they rob; the grander the premises, the bigger the 'job'. Many professional burglars scorn this disagreeable legend, as it obviously devalues their social and criminal status. A famous case of detection by turd took place a few years ago in the Liverpool district known as 'Spike Island'. A gang of small-time housebreakers had been rounded up and taken to the local police station. All but one confessed; and he was finally convicted because a turd had been found on the dressing-table bearing a perfect thumb-print that matched his own. No evidence was offered that the deposit was that of the accused; but the defence did not dispute the matter.

(See also Copraphilia)

Exhumation

Exactly what happens to a dead body in a coffin has exercised many morbid imaginations – not least those of Edgar Allan Poe and Charles Dickens. During Dickens' first visit to America in 1842, the two writers spent many evenings together drinking heavily and discussing the physical phenomena of the after-death.

The subject also arouses great curiosity, even speculation, among scientists and medical men, since the occasion on which the contents of a long-buried coffin can be examined at leisure are rare, for obvious reasons. Such opportunities usually occur only when the police suspect foul play and a court orders the body to be exhumed. One such case was that of Mrs Beryl Evans and her eighteen-month old baby Geraldine, whose bodies were exhumed in the wake of the Christie Murders. Mrs Evans' husband, Timothy had been hanged two years earlier, in 1950, for the murder of both his wife and daughter – crimes for which he was posthumously pardoned. John Reginald Halliday Christie who had been the chief prosecution witness against Evans at his trial in 1949, was later found to have committed at least nine other murders – including those of Mrs Evans and her baby daughter.

The exhumation of the two bodies, and their subsequent examination, are described in detail by the Home Office pathologist, the late Prof. Francis Camps, in his work *Medical and Scientific Evidence in the Christie Case* (1953). He records that the coffin, containing both bodies, was the top one of six in a common grave. The exhumation took place before dawn; the coffin lid was slightly raised and left, under police guard, for a couple of hours in order to allow the gases to escape. It was then taken to Kensington Mortuary where the lid was removed, 'to show the two bodies covered with a shroud which was fairly heavily overgrown with a whitish coloured mould. This also hung down in stalactites from the inside of the coffin lid. The bodies were clearly outlined beneath the shroud, which was adherent and friable, and when this was stripped off they were seen to be in a remarkably good condition from the point of view of identification by reason of adipocere formation.' (See Decomposition)

The body of Mrs Evans was lying on wet sawdust which was brown and somewhat damp, although there was no free water in the coffin, and the face was almost recognisable – a remarkable fact, according to Camps. He also noted at this stage there was very little smell. The colouration of Mrs Evans' body and tissues were 'white-yellow and the muscle was bleached. The tissue cut very firmly with the consistency of ''cured bacon'' and was somewhat greasy to touch.' The child's body, resting on the mother's, was almost black.

Eye-lashes

Alluring false eye-lashes worn to enhance personal and sexual attraction tend to have an adverse effect when found, detached from their wearer, on the pillow next morning. Less common now is the use of goat's eye-lashes as a sex aid. In thirteenth century Tibet, when a goat had been killed, its eye-lids – complete with eye-lashes – were dried and then steamed several times. This 'happy ring' was then fastened round the penis.

A rare medical condition, distichiasis, is the appearance of a double row of eye-lashes on one or both eye-lids.

Factory Farming

The conditions in which chickens are kept in broiler houses are without doubt disgusting: crammed into cages, their necks rubbed bare, fed on fish-meal – and so is the meat which results from this treatment.

An investigative journalist just back from India has informed the authors of a new and hopefully unique refinement: simultaneous factory farming of chickens and prawns. A multi-national company has set up a system of water-tanks seeded with prawn roe over which wire-bottomed chicken cages are suspended. The chicken-shit falls into the prawn tanks providing their only source of nourishment. When both chickens and prawns have reached a passable state of maturity, they are frozen and exported to gullible gourmets in the West.

Fartleberries

According to the admirable Mr Eric Partridge, these
are 'excrement on the anal hair,' low English, late
eighteenth to nineteenth century. In modern times,
there is no comparable description; but fartleberries
are a familiar nuisance to hospital nurses, particularly
those dealing with tramps and down-and-outs.
Especially common to very hairy men (and women),
they present a problem prior to operations on or
around the anus, usually for piles, when the offending
tufts have to be cut away, usually with nail-scissors.

Fartleberries also played an important role in the
apprehension and conviction of the Great Train
Robbers in 1963. Vital forensic evidence, found in the
cess-pit under Leatherslade Farm, included
individual anal hairs which had been detached from
their owners by the abrasive scouring of lavatory
paper against obstinate fartleberries. Samples were
matched with those belonging to several members of
the gang, and were later produced as evidence at
Aylesbury Crown Court.

Fawn-tail

A congenital abnormality of the spine causes a number of babies to be born with a vestigial tail of bone and cartilage protruding from the base of the spine and covered with downy hair. Unless it is removed, it can prevent the development of the spinal cord and cause disorders of the bladder and bowels.

However, in the past, fawn tails were looked upon as sexually arousing and courtesans in Parisian brothels who possessed 'la petite queue' were in great demand.

A Turkish army recruit was found to have a tail sixteen inches long and two inches in diameter. He managed to keep it hidden until his medical examination. It was decided not to cut a hole in his uniform trousers but to keep the tail hidden because of its vulnerability in action.

Fibroids

Non-malignant lumps of muscular and fibrous tissue attached to the womb and ranging in size from small pimples to lumps twice the size of a football weighing several pounds. Fibroids are also known as 'womb stones' since, if not removed, they may become calcified.

However, surgery is not necessary unless the womb becomes abnormally distended or the fibroids press on the bowels or bladder causing digestive disorders or involuntary emptying of the bladder. Fibroids can also cause heavy menstrual periods during which clots of blood, described by a leading London gynaecologist as 'lumps of liver', are expelled.

Fish Pie

A distinguished professor at one of our older universities received a telephone call from his wife, reminding him that they were expecting dinner guests that night and asking him to buy a frozen fish pie from a nearby supermarket. He did as asked but, being proverbially absent-minded, returned home without it. What, if anything, their guests ate that night is not recorded.

The matter passed from his mind until, some six weeks later, one of the professor's colleagues opened a little-used drawer in his own desk, in which were kept some extremely valuable prints by such artists as Leonardo da Vinci and Raphael. Nestling among these works of art was the fish pie, by this time extremely noisome and active. 'So that's where I put it!' said the professor.

Flatulence

> The ancient Pelusians did (amongst other whimsical, chimerical objects of veneration and worship) venerate a Fart, which they worshipped under the symbol of a swelled paunch.
>
> Charles Percy: *A View of the Levant* (1743)

The innumerable bacteria (*qv*) which inhabit the intestines (*qv*) produce marsh gas and hydrogen when food is digested. Certain foods such as beans, onions, Jerusalem artichokes and potato chips increase flatulence – even such delicacies as champagne and souffles.

In the United States alone, nine million cubic feet of intestinal gas are expelled each day; apart from the embarrassment they cause, farts have many potential uses which have yet to be harnessed. Research is currently being carried out in New Zealand into ways of recycling sheep farts, known as 'biogas'. Since each of New Zealand's seventy million sheep produces twenty litres of wind per day, their combined farting power could prove a major source of energy. The only problem is how to collect such a valuable commodity; for controversy has already arisen over whether all the gas is expelled through the sheep's nether regions or whether a considerable percentage leaves through the mouth.

Nervousness is well known as a cause of diarrhoea (comedian Billy Connolly described it as 'the best laxative I know') but it can also result in flatulence. A pretty young fashion model was invited out to dinner by a leading photographer, as well known for the speed of his seductions as for his success in persuading top magazines to use his work. Awed by the implications and possibilities of their tête-à-tête, the model was seized with a desire to fart just as the photographer rang her doorbell.

Ushering her into the passenger seat of his expensive car, he noticed a wine shop across the road offering chilled champagne and hurried over to buy some. At last, the model had a chance to expel the lingering pocket of air from her bowels. Having been contained for so long, it emerged with a satisfying roar. Seconds later, the photographer returned.

'Oh, sorry, I forgot to introduce you.'

Aghast, the model turned her head. In the back seat, faintly lit by the street light, was another couple.

The French music-hall fartist known as Le Petomane put his talent to good use at the Folies Bergère where he was top of the bill in the 1890s and even gave a private performance for the Prince of Wales. A female rival was found to be a fraud, concealing whistles and trumpets under her bustle and voluminous skirts. Le Petomane, a true performer to the end, is said to have farted the tune of 'The Last Post' on his deathbed.

Flies

The fly likes to lay its eggs – up to six hundred at a time – in meat, preferably rotting. Within forty-eight hours, the maggots hatch and start burrowing into their fleshy habitat. Once developed, the fly paddles about with its hairy legs in excrement, meaty putrescence and other filth, and then settles on food. Not only are bacteria carried on its feet, legs and body, but while eating the fly repeatedly vomits and then re-swallows its food, mashing the resulting goo with its filthy feet before doing so.

Foot-binding

Tan-ke, Empress of China in the eleventh century BC, was born with club feet and forced her husband to issue a law ordering all girls' feet to be bound to the shape of her own. After her death, the custom may have waned but foot-binding was certainly popular among dancing girls of the T'ang period, and continued to be widely practised in China well into the twentieth century.

A British officer who served in China between the wars remembered the screams of young girls who received this treatment, and his daughter – who spent some years in China in the 1940s – recalls hobbling along behind old women, imitating their halting movements with all the cruelty of childhood.

However, the rolling gait of women with bound feet was thought extremely attractive by Chinese men, and 'natural-footed' women could only hope to be taken as second wives, little better than slaves. The name suggests that the feet were simply bound tightly to stunt their growth but the actual process was far more painful.

Young girls, aged about five or six, had the four smaller toes of each foot bent downwards and tightly bound. Then the foot was arched, the heel and toes bound together. Finally, the big toe was curved inwards and bound. Through walking – or hobbling – the child's own weight would break the bones of the feet which would then reset within the tight binding and eventually become only a few inches long.

Funeral Fashions

What to wear to a funeral is a problem for the fashion-conscious mourner but the guest of honour – the corpse – has a wide variety of clothes from which to choose. Specially-designed suits, dresses, negligees and even shoes are described by Jessica Mitford in *The American Way of Death*. Quoting from the catalogue of the Practical Burial Footwear Company of Columbus, Ohio, she cites the 'Fit-A-Fut Oxford' – available in a variety of colours – or the 'Ko-Zee' slipper with 'soft, cushioned soles and warm, luxurious slipper comfort, but true shoe smartness'. No doubt the corpse is grateful for the warmth, comfort and smartness of its footwear.

For women, the 'New Bra-Form, Post Mortem Form Restoration' brassiere is vital, especially for wearing under one of the selection of hostess gowns and brunch coats manufactured by Florence Gowns Inc.

Not all corpses are so lucky. When Dorothy Parker and Alan Campbell divorced for the second time (her comment on their remarriage was 'Brideshead Revisited'!), Campbell shared an apartment with an old friend from college days. Life was hard for the two men, both out of work, short of money and drinking heavily. Campbell returned from a trip one day to find his friend had dropped dead from alcoholic poisoning and was already in the hands of the mortician. The burial had to be hasty and cheap since there was no spare cash available. Only later, when summoned to an important meeting, did Campbell realise that his best suit was missing. So were his only good shirt, tie, and smart shoes. His friend had been buried in them.

While Dylan Thomas was 'reposing' in a New York funeral parlour after his early death induced by drinking 18 straight whiskeys, a friend contemplated the poet's vulgar funeral suit and commented: 'He would never have been seen dead in that!'

Giggle Micturition

The complete emptying of the bladder, caused by

helpless laughter. In 1937, a very beautiful but inexperienced actress appeared as the female lead in a Noël Coward play at a London theatre. Her costume for the first scene was a tight white satin dress. In her nervousness on the first night, she laughed uncontrollably at the leading man's lines and – without noticing – urinated while sitting on a sofa. Unfortunately, her exit through the French windows had to be made with her back to the audience who were left in no doubt as to the cause of the large stain on the back of her costume.

Goldfish, Unusual uses for
See Vagina

Gonorrhea

Many have claimed that the strictures of Victorian morality have their roots as much in the terror of gonorrhea, or 'pox' as it was called, as in any virtuous standards of religious or moral propriety. This terror of the disease is well documented by the admirable Mr James Boswell in his *London Journal (1762-1763)*. Having conceived a great passion for an actress, Mrs Louisa Lewis, and having consummated his passion several times, he woke one morning to find

'the poisonous infection raging in my veins. What! thought I, can this beautiful, this sensible, and this agreeable woman be so sadly defiled? Can corruption lodge beneath so fair a form? Can she who professed delicacy of sentiment and sincere regard for me, use me so very basely and so very cruelly? No, it is impossible. I have just got a gleet by irritating the parts too much with excessive venery. And yet these damned twinges, that scalding heat, and that deep-tinged loathsome matter are the strongest proofs of an infection. But perhaps she was ignorant of her being ill. A pretty conjecture indeed! No, she could not be ignorant ...

Not one to beat about the bush, Boswell confronted the young lady that same day. He recorded that she 'turned pale as ashes and trembled and faltered.' For those who think of the eighteenth century as an age of chivalry, Boswell makes clear that what irritated him even more than being 'laid up for many weeks to suffer extreme pain and full confinement, and to be debarred all the comforts and pleasures of life,' was the fact that he had lent this 'consummate dissembling whore' *two guineas*!

A week later he wrote to her:

MADAM: My surgeon will soon have demand upon me for curing the disease which you have given me. I must therefore remind you of the sum which you had of me sometime ago. I give you notice that I expect to have it before Saturday sennight (week). Call not that a misfortune which is the consequence of your own unworthiness. I desire no mean evasions. I want no letters. Send the money sealed up. I have nothing to say to you.

Exactly one week later, Louisa returned the money. 'I was glad that I had come off two guineas better than I expected,' this chivalrous libertine noted in his Journal.

There are certain people who make a virtue of venereal disease. One of the authors knows a former member of the Australian Naval Reserve who, while on board HMAS Supply, was invited to participate in a competition to see who would be the first to catch the clap from the Kings Cross prostitutes in Sydney.

A leading war correspondent for an international news magazine was proud of the number of times he had contracted gonorrhea during his world travels and used to boast openly that several of the strains he had picked up – notably the Congo and Biafra – were incurable.

In the mid-Sixties his appearance in Saigon caused consternation among fellow journalists covering the war. At the time, the correspondent in question was claiming to have caught the clap no less than forty-nine times. His body was harbouring at least four incurable strains which were defying all known antibiotics.

In those days Saigon still retained some of its easy French Colonial charm before the influx of the licentious American soldiery. The more discerning journalists had discovered a discreet bordello which they nicknamed 'The Strategic Brothel' because it was across the road from the radio station, giving journalists a grandstand view of the latest military coup. The girls were all sixth-formers from the local French lycée and could engage their clients in intelligent conversation about modern French literature. This ideal combination of sexual and intellectual stimulation and local politics was too good to last. One day, a British correspondent entered the bar of Saigon's main hotel with the dreadful news that our hero had been seen leaving The Strategic Brothel. The rest of the press corps never crossed its threshold again, fearing that they would catch one of the many strains of gonorrhea which infested his body.

These strains included one that had been nicknamed 'Saigon Rose' on account of the lurid inflammation it caused. Another was the 'Da Nang Special,' common among the U.S. Marine Corps, one of whose number – Captain Homer Nelson – was known as Nelson the Nail. He described his symptoms to one of the authors: 'I used to weigh two hundred and fifty pounds without a hard on. Since I picked up this cruddy disease, my dick has been burning away like a candle – it's half its normal length and as thin as a nail. Now I can't get a hard-on at all and I have to keep it wrapped in surgical dressing.'

Our war correspondent, undeterred, continued to spread his own particular brand of goodwill around the world.

Halitosis

Unpleasant, foetid breath caused by gum infections, indigestion, and certain illnesses such as ozoena which also causes crusts to appear around the nose.

Perhaps the most potent description of halitosis is also one of the earliest, by that observant Dutch microscopist Antony van Leeuwenhoek. In 1683 he wrote:-

There are more animals living in the scum of the teeth in a man's mouth than there are men in a whole kingdom especially in those who don't ever clean their teeth, whereby such a stench comes from the mouth of many of 'em that you can scarcely bear to talk to them; which is called by many people 'having a stinking breath' though in sooth 'tis most always a stinking *mouth*

See also Plaque.

Hermaphrodites

Few cases of true, or gonadal, hermaphrodites have been recorded in medical history. Also known as intersexuality and not to be confused with trans-sexualism (*qv*), this is caused by a disorder in the development of the genitals during the growth of the foetus. Normally, the baby's sex can be distinguished by the end of the fourth month of pregnancy but hermaphrodites are born with ovotestes – a combination of ovaries and testicles.

Outwardly, hermaphrodites appear to be either the male or female gender but 'males' are likely to have undescended testicles, developed breasts and a displaced urethra while 'females' have an abnormally developed clitoris resembling a penis.

Herpes

The menace of herpes has recently been overshadowed by AIDS, but it remains an extremely unpleasant condition which can recur indefinitely.

There are three types of herpes: *Herpes simplex*, commonly known as cold sores, which usually appear on the mouth and lips causing pain, irritation and hideous rough, red patches. Scrum-pox is a variety of this virus.

Herpes zoster, or shingles, is an extremely painful affliction very much like chicken-pox. A ring of yellow pustules appear round the chest, itching intensely and eventually bursting, forming scabs. Sometimes a group of pustules coagulates and forms a 'bleb' which may ulcerate and leave a scar. Even when the pustules have disappeared, the painful itching may remain.

However, it is *Genital herpes* which made the cover of *Time* Magazine and was the most fashionable sexually transmitted disease until AIDS took centre stage, although it had, in fact, been around for two million years. It has increased ten-fold over the last ten years and some 300,000 new cases are diagnosed in the

United States alone each year; since it is virtually incurable, the total number of sufferers runs into millions.

The first sign of herpes is burning, itchy pain – on the penis in men and the outer lips of the vagina in women – followed by red, painful spots which rapidly become blisters filled with clear pus. This soon turns yellow and the blisters burst. Ulcers then form, covered with scabs, which take up to two weeks to heal. It is during and shortly after this healing period that the infection is most likely to be passed on, since the pain during an attack is so distressing that the sufferer is unlikely to have sexual contact.

However, infection can be carried on the hands and even on shared towels or clothing. Also, oral or anal sexual contact can spread the virus to other parts of the body. Although the first attack of herpes is the worst, it can recur indefinitely, sometimes triggered off by stress or hormonal changes such as menstruation (*qv*).

It is interesting to note that 99 per cent of prostitutes have anti-bodies to the genital herpes virus in their blood while only 3 per cent of nuns are so protected.

Intestines

Up to thirty feet of intestines – almost half the length of a tennis court – are coiled within the human abdomen. Food is churned through this succession of narrow tubes after leaving the stomach, broken down by pancreatic and intestinal juices and by the millions of bacteria which inhabit the intestines (also known as the bowels). Among these is *Clostridium welchii* which causes the rapid spread of gas gangrene in war wounds and which can grow only without oxygen, preferring dead or damaged flesh as its habitat. However, in a healthy body they cause no harm.

Foodies may like to know that, according to cookery writer Glynn Christian, the ideal casing for a salami is the cleansed intestine of a pig. Apparently, each part of the intestine contains different sorts of bacteria and enzymes and thus gives a different flavour to the salami. As if that wasn't enough some salami makers go even further. The *saucisson* called Rose de Lyon isn't named after its colour: the casing is made from the last few feet of the pig's large intestine – and its sphincter. *Bon appetit!*

Janiceps

Also known as diprosopus, a foetus with two faces and one head. In certain cases, rather than having two séparate sets of eyes, the two eyes nearest the centre of the skull occupy the same socket, giving a 'double Cyclops' effect.

Jigger

A colloquial term for the parasitic sand-flea. Also used to describe the small worm-like deposits of fatty excrescence which can be squeezed out of the sebaceous glands. See also Acne.

Kuru

A slow and fatal disease attacking the nervous system, caused by cannibalism – particularly by eating the brains of deceased relatives in the Highlands of New Guinea where such practices used to be common, particularly among women and children.

Lavatory Paper

A major paper manufacturer recently announced sales of two and a half million rolls of lavatory paper per day in Britain. If it were used throughout the world in the same quantity, every wood and forest on the planet would be denuded to the last tree within three years.

Quality varies: until a few years ago, 'Bronco' paper was popular in Britain; it somehow managed to combine the qualities of being both shiny and abrasive. Similar paper used in official institutions was stamped 'Government Property', sometimes alternated with the terse command 'Now Wash Your Hands'. Some people still prefer the spartan quality of 'hard' lavatory paper to the soft option of tissue.

However, before the introduction of manufactured lavatory paper, a number of less satisfactory alternatives were used: stones, leaves, fingers – or nothing. Sir Roger l'Estrange reported that King James I enjoyed hunting so much that 'he would not leave the saddle even to relieve himself, so that his servants had a pretty mess to clean up at the day's end'.

In his fascinating book *Scatalogic Rites of All Nations* published in 1891, J.G. Bourke describes the Roman habit of keeping a sponge tied to a stick in a bucket of salt water with which 'the passer by cleansed his person, and then replaced the stick in the tub'.

In Medieval times, clumps of hay known as *mempiria* were used but a less prickly alternative was a specially-designed tool, rather like a hockey stick in shape, with which the last vestiges of excrement could be scraped off. This may explain the origin of the phrase 'grasping the wrong end of the stick'.

Leeches

Leeches are coming back into fashion for medical use, to draw off small quantities of blood during surgery. They were especially popular with doctors during the seventeenth century when blood-letting was the fashionable cure-all, killing off many people who might otherwise have survived into old age.

Although small, leeches become distended with blood and are extremely difficult to detach once clamped on to their prey with their sharp teeth and sucker-shaped mouth. Applying a lighted cigarette to their rear end results in a messy but effective explosion.

The well-known writer Brian Aldiss spent the war years in the Far East – described in his excellent novel *A Soldier Erect* – where he grappled with leeches, as well as various other types of local fauna. On his first day off, he attended a cricket match and was puzzled to see all the spectators standing although there were rows of empty seats. As soon as he sat down, he discovered why: hordes of hungry leeches converged on him from the undergrowth. More than forty years later he still carries a scar.

Legionnaires' Disease

So called because it was first identified when it struck a group of members of the American Legion holding a reunion at a hotel in Philadelphia – not, as is often thought, because of a more romantic association with the French Foreign Legion.

The symptoms are similar to those of pneumonia and the spread of the bacillus is encouraged by the trappings of civilisation; it is found most frequently in air-conditioning systems and humidifiers. A recent survey showed that the bacillus flourishes in all the hotels and hospitals tested in Britain, and that the larger the establishment, the greater is the density of the bacteria, irrespective – in the case of hotels and private hospitals – of the size of the bill rendered to the inmates.

This is a small example of the alarming statistic that up to 50 per cent of patients have to be treated for infections picked up on hospital premises. Doctors and hospital administrators attempt to deny this – but they would, wouldn't they?

Legs, length of

A number of cosmetic operations are available for improving the aesthetic quality of the lower limbs, including the 'Lipolsysis operation' which involves the re-contouring of the area round hips, buttocks, abdomen and thighs rather in the manner of Capability Brown's recontouring of landscapes in the eighteenth century. The cost is approximately that of a return trip from London to New York on Concorde.

A statuesque Scandinavian starlet in the '60's, trying to carve out a film career for herself in Rome, had four inches of thigh-bone removed from each leg in order to measure up to her Italian admirers.

A jealous rival later started the malicious rumour that the discarded shards of the thigh-bone had been served up as *osso buco* at a fashionable dinner party in a villa near Rome.

Lice

Head-lice thrive in warm, moist conditions. Even regular shampooing does not guarantee freedom from this parasite which spreads rapidly in schools and other places where towels, combs and hair-brushes are shared. 25,000 people a day in the United States discover that they have lice. There are similar alarming statistics in Britain where there are 3,000 per cent more cases of lice in schools now than there were 20 years ago.

During World War II, the bomb shelters in London's underground stations provided excellent breeding grounds. The bunks which were at one time installed in them had to be removed because of infestation.

Lice are not only found on humans. A recent nostalgic correspondence in the *Daily Telegraph* about the delights of eating rook pie were marred by one correspondent's memory that his hands were 'covered with lice' after cleaning the rooks.

Lower down the scale, crab lice are regular inhabitants of pubic hair and some 10,000 patients a year report to Britain's VD clinics suffering from them. A photographer told one of the authors that, on his way to an assignment in a large London hotel, he wanted to have 'a really good scratch' in the lift as he knew he wouldn't have a chance to relieve the itching while at work. He had just opened his flies and squeezed his hand into his underpants when the lift door flew open and a crowd of smartly-dressed ladies surged into the lift. Purple with embarrassment, the photographer collected his equipment and fled, but not before the lift had swept him ten floors past his destination.

Lichen

Chronic papules or suppurating pimples, caused by habitual scratching or emotional stress, particularly in women. Usually lichen appears on the nape of the neck and sometimes on the inner part of the thigh. In extreme cases, after the papules have dried out, the skin becomes hardened, even cracked, and resembles in appearance and texture Morocco leather.

The disease has sometimes been known to spread over the whole body and even inside the mouth.

Lick Eczema

Common among children who habitually suck their thumbs – a wet inflammation which erupts round the mouth – caused by the constant soaking of the skin in dirty saliva.

Lithopaedion

The medical term for a foetus which dies in its mother's body and becomes calcified. In 1985 the foetus of a child conceived in 1924 was found in the body of an eighty-five-year old woman. Some years ago, a British gynaecologist working in Aden discovered a calcified foetus in the body of an Arab woman. Some years previously she had apparently become pregnant and gone into labour but no child emerged so it was thought she had suffered a phantom pregnancy. Only later was it discovered that her womb had burst during labour and the foetus had shot into her abdomen where it died, and was found as a shrunken petrified lump pressing against the wall of her stomach.

Liver

The liver is a particularly tough organ. It can sustain large amounts of punishment from excessive alcohol from which it usually recovers after a period of abstention. Liver damage comes in four stages, of which only the last two are irreparable, and the final one fatal.

In the early part of this century such examples of fourth-stage cirrhosis were trophies much prized by medical men. Shortly after the First World War, a young surgeon, Jack Carus-Wilson, later to become the head of St Bartholomew's Hospital, stood over the body of an old woman from Limehouse who was dying of cirrhosis. He gave the following instructions to his students: 'As soon as she goes, I want that liver.' It was duly extracted wrapped up in a piece of newspaper, and he took it home with him on the bus. Being an absent-minded man, he arrived home without his parcel. The fate of the diseased liver must be left to the imagination; but it can be safely assumed that some member of the deserving poor classes, seeing a well-dressed man leaving behind a piece of meat wrapped in newspaper, would have taken it home without further thought, and cooked it for his dinner.

Lupus

A particularly unsightly skin disease is *Lupus vulgaris*; the first sign of this persistent and night-marish illness is an 'apple jelly' nodule, so called because it is transparent and yellow. The skin thickens and gradually becomes covered with nodules which ulcerate and form abscesses (*qv*). The face and neck are especially vulnerable to lupus which, even when successfully treated in one area, may reappear in another. Eventually, the nose may be partly or even completely eaten away and the lower eyelids are drawn down, showing their red rims.

Masturbation

Achieving orgasm through self-induced friction. Perhaps the most drastic form of masturbation was

90

practised by the man who put his penis into the tube of a vacuum cleaner which he then switched on. He used this method only once. Only two or three men in a thousand can reach orgasm through sucking their own penises. Kinsey noted in his famous *Report* that some women masturbated over a hundred times in an hour and that, in general, women masturbate more often than men.

During the Vietnam War, the incidence of venereal disease became so threatening that, in the words of a senior Australian television broadcaster, 'You can't even masturbate in this country without using a rubber glove'.

Voltaire, on his death bed, confessed to having masturbated each day of his life. Whether he had shown the precosity of the seven-month old baby observed masturbating by Kinsey is not known.

Methods of masturbation vary. A young doctor recently told one of the authors that, while on casualty duty, he treated a man admitted with a tomato ketchup bottle irremovably stuck in his anus. His explanation was that he had been to the supermarket and forgotten his keys. While climbing to an upstairs window up a drain-pipe, his trousers came down. Trying to hoist them up, he fell, landing on the bottle of ketchup which was sticking out of his carrier bag on the ground below. His story might have carried more clout if the bottle – still full of ketchup – had not had a condom over the end.

Meat Baths

Kaiser Leopold I of Austria was born, in 1640, two months prematurely. As Beethoven was later told by his journalist friend Carl Bernard, Leopold was repeatedly put into a freshly-slaughtered pig to help him gain strength. The meat was later given to the poor who called it *Kaiserfleisch*. This name is now given to an Austrian delicacy of lightly-smoked pork.

Schumann, who suffered from stiffness in his right hand, was advised in the 1830s to dabble it in the warm entrails, faeces and blood of a newly-killed calf, pig or lamb. We do not know whether this remedy worked or who ate the unfortunate animals used for the cure.

Mendicants

The Mendicity Society, in the nineteenth century, tried to clear London's streets of fake cripples (see 'Scaldrum Dodge'). However, in *London Labour and the London Poor*, his encyclopedic survey published in the mid-nineteenth century, Henry Mayhew noted:-

> Various kinds of cripples are still to be found, begging in the streets of London. The public will be familiar with the personal appearance of many of them. There is the crab-like man without legs, who sits strapped to a board and walks upon his

hands; the legless man who propels himself in a little carriage, constructed on the velocipede principle. I cannot think, however, that the police exercise a wise discretion in permitting some of the more hideous of these beggars to infest the streets. Instances are on record of nervous females having been seriously frightened, and even injured, by seeing men without legs or arms crawling at their feet.

A case is within my own knowledge, where the sight of a man without legs or arms had such an effect upon a lady in the family way that her child was born in all respects the very counterpart of the object that alarmed her. It had neither legs nor arms.

Some fake cripples were still at large:

His right sleeve hung loose at his side, and there appeared to be nothing left of his arm but a short stump. On being examined at the police office his arm was found strapped to his side, and the stump turned out to be a stuffing of bran.

Among other fake mendicants Mayhew encountered was one described as 'An Author's Wife' who attempted to sell him in a tavern, a printed sheet entitled 'The Pretty Girls of London' which purported to be part of a book which her invalid husband was writing. Mayhew objected to the 'morality' of the section he read, to which the 'Author's Wife' replied: 'But's that's what it takes, sir.' It turned out that her 'husband' was not really the author of 'The Pretty Girls of London' but a notorious begging-letter writer. The methods used by the 'Author's Wife' might well be revived by the spouses of present-day writers.

Menstruation

The lining of the womb, also known as the endometrium, detaches itself and flows out gradually through the vagina approximately once every twenty-eight days. Menstruation can take as little as two days or as long as eight, and is accompanied by hormonal changes in the body which account for the pre-menstrual syndrome – though many women find the emotional as well as physical effects of menstruation last throughout their 'period'. Other synonyms include 'the curse', 'being off games' and 'a bloody waste of fucking time'. The French, more historically-minded, sometimes use the phrase 'les anglais s'embarquent', no doubt drawing the analogy with the red coats worn by British soldiers during the Napoleonic Wars.

Even normal menstruation is unpleasant, both for the woman concerned and for those around her if she does not change her tampons or pads frequently since once menstrual blood is exposed to the air it has a peculiarly cloying and unpleasant smell. Dysmenorrhea, or painful menstruation, has symptoms such as cramps in the back and abdomen, nausea, diarrhoea (*qv*) and clots appearing in the menstrual blood (see Fibroids).

Females menstruate for some one thousand eight hundred days between puberty and menopause, and use about eight thousand tampons or sanitary pads during that time.

Mercury Poisoning

Detectives who use dusting powder to disclose finger-prints may not realise that mercury is one of its ingredients and that constant use can lead to chronic mercury poisoning. The first signs are halitosis (*qv*), bleeding gums and swollen tongue. Eventually, the teeth fall out and the jaw becomes infected.

Mercury has been used in the production of felt hats; another symptom of poisoning is known as 'hatter's shakes'. It also leads to erethism, a psychological condition whose victims suffer from resentment of criticism, shyness, indecision and depression and which explains the origin of the phrase 'as mad as a hatter'.

Acute mercury poisoning, caused by swallowing this substance or a compound of it such as a fungicide, usually leads to rapid death after burning pain, diarrhoea, and vomiting; the lips and mouth are burned white.

Mould

A fungus growth, which can either be dry or damp, of

a grey, pale green or whitish colour which grows on dead or decaying matter, including corpses.

In the notorious Christie case in 1952 (see Putrefaction and Necrophilia) one of the last victims, a young prostitute whose half-naked body was discovered in the cupboard of 10 Rillington Place, was found to be remarkably well-preserved – except for what was described in the official report as 'a tusk of white mould protruding from the left nostril.'

Necrophilia

Love of the dead – or, more specifically, those who prefer sexual intercourse with corpses. Two celebrated murderers in Britain since the Second World War have drawn attention to this peculiar proclivity: George Reginald Halliday Christie who, in 1952, was hanged after murdering at least nine women whose bodies he kept concealed about the house or buried in the garden of 10 Rillington Place near London's Ladbroke Grove (see Exhumation). The other was Dennis Nilsen who was sentenced in 1983 to life imprisonment for the murder of no fewer than fifteen young men whose bodies he had dismembered, boiled or burned.

Both men were not only seedy, self-righteous and dreary in the extreme but were, on the surface, 'of exemplary character', both efficient and officious. Both, at some time in their careers, had been policemen and both led outwardly respectable lives. Christie was a diligent railway clerk, Nilsen a civil servant working in an employment centre. Both committed their murders with fastidious attention to detail. Christie gassed his victims and had intercourse with them after death; he kept their bodies concealed in cupboards and would bring them out at intervals, when he used to enjoy them without fear of being mocked for his sexual inadequacy; his attentions ceased only when the condition of the bodies rendered them unserviceable.

Nilsen, a man of repressed homosexual tastes, claims never to have actually penetrated the bodies of his young down-and-out victims. He preferred instead to masturbate over them or to rub himself off between their thighs. His case is a catalogue of genteel horrors, all committed at two respectable addresses in Muswell Hill, North London. His victims were strangled, then carefully washed in the bath if they had vomited or defecated before or during death. They were then usually hung up by their ankles. Photographed and contemplated at leisure before being carved up with a butcher's skill, boiled in saucepans and disposed of in suitcases and plastic bags. Sections of their bodies, with their rotting stomach contents, were also flushed down the lavatory – which eventually led to Nilsen's arrest.

Nilsen's own meticulous account of his crimes, as related to Brian Masters in his book *Killing for Company*, revealed that these murders were committed at gruesome leisure, usually to the accompaniment of taped music and reflected by mirrors. Nilsen chain-smoked and mixed strong drinks while carrying out his obsessional pastime, and also had frequent baths. Throughout, his only witness was Bleep, his mongrel bitch, whose demeanour the murderer described as 'a bit sheepish'. Like Christie, Nilsen used large quantities of disinfectant to disguise the smell and keep down the maggots.

Although the Nilsen case attracted the usual plethora of benign clap-trap from psychologists and sociologists in search of explanatory excuses for this atrocious creature, Nilsen's personality was perhaps best summed up – with typically outrageous insight – by Auberon Waugh who described him as a typical minor civil servant who, working within the 'caring' public sector, was so boring that the only way he could persuade people to endure his company was by killing them and keeping their corpses around the house.

Christie remains an altogether superior figure in the annals of crime, both as murderer and necro-philiac – not least because, while still a police officer, he also murdered the wife and baby daughter of his lodger and later gave damning evidence against him which led to his wrongful execution.

A number of books, and a major film starring Richard Attenborough, have already commemorated the Christie case but regretfully, so far, no attempt has been made to launch the musical which it inspired, entitled 'Corpus Christie'. Song titles from this show include 'Underneath the Floorboards'; 'There are Femurs at the Bottom of my Garden'; 'Cupboard Love'; 'Fanny by Gaslight' and 'Thank Evans for Little Girls'. It is doubtful whether the Nilsen case will ever inspire such creative ventures.

Nose-picking

Public nose-picking appears to be on the increase. Drivers stuck in traffic jams seem particularly prone to this repellant habit, apparently forgetting that the windows of their car afford no protection from the gaze of passers-by.

An unappetising by-product of nose-picking is practised by those who eat the results of their excavations. Why? For the answer, see Snot.

Obesity

Excessive body fat caused by disturbance of the endocrine glands and by over-indulgence and inactivity. Daniel Lambert, the heaviest man who ever lived, weighed 739 lbs (335 kg). He died at the age of 39 in 1809 and his specially-constructed chair may be seen at Peterborough Museum.

Obesity occurs more often in women than in men and leads to general poor health and such embarrassments as chafing of the skin where the two skin surfaces (such as inner thighs) meet.

An extreme example of the dangers of obesity occurred recently in a small town in Yugoslavia where a man was trapped for three days under his 275-pound wife after she suffered a fatal heart attack as they were going up to bed. The husband, who weighed only 119 lbs, was knocked unconscious when his wife fell on him and revived to find himself pinned down by her weight, his hip broken. He remained trapped, without food or drink except water from a vase of flowers, until discovered 60 hours later by a passing postman.

Oral Sex

Known by the charming Latin nomenclaturae, *fellatio* and *cunnilingus*. Fellatio is the application of the mouth and tongue to the penis; cunnilingus, of the tongue to the clitoris and vulvae. In certain states of America, particularly the Bible Belt and the South, oral sex is a crime punishable by long prison sentences. In Florida, such activities are described on the statute book as 'abominable crimes against Nature'.

Moral censure apart, there are compelling medical reasons to support this. In the last few years, at least two deaths have been reported in Britain and a larger number in the United States, resulting from air being blown into the vagina and causing an embolism followed rapidly by death. It is not known if this is the origin of the phrase 'blow-job'.

Even in Britain today, oral sex against the partner's wishes is still recognised as grounds for divorce. In a famous case, the late Mr Justice Salmon interrupted a woman testifying against her husband for forcing her into depraved and unnatural practices – viz. fellatio against her will – by asking, 'Madam, have you no teeth?'

Although some women positively enjoy male ejaculation into the mouth, on the whole it is regarded as a disagreeable experience, since the sudden flood of semen has 'the taste and consistency of a mouthful of tepid, fishy porridge'.

In a notorious scandal in Italy in the 1950s, leading to the resignation of a Cabinet Minister, the body of a seventeen year-old girl was dumped in a suburb of Rome after she had choked to death on a mouthful of semen during an orgy at which most of Italy's *dolce vita* society were present. Oral sex was also the source of the only publicised sex scandal in the Communist bloc. Orgies were held in a villa outside Budapest at which a number of air hostesses from East European airlines were entertained by top Communist officials. Typically, the Hungarians combined the pleasures of fellatio and cunnilingus with exotic gastronomic delights. Orifices and organs were plentifully smeared with sour cream, Russian caviar and various flavours of succulent Hungarian jam. No deaths resulted, although several party *apparatchki* spent the next few years on a prison diet.

Perhaps significantly, a leading luminary of the British establishment who is himself of Austro-Hungarian origin recently boasted to a friend: 'I am the Nijinsky of cunnilingus'.

Oriental Sore

Also known as Delhi Boil, Aleppo Boil or Biskra Button, this is caused by parasites lodging under the skin in clusters which grow to the size and shape of a lemon. If the 'boil' is lanced, thousands of tiny *Leishmania donovani* – as these parasites are known – spill out in a heaving mass. In certain cases they eat into cartilage and cause erosion of the nose.

Ovarian Cysts

Ovarian cysts reach enormous size. The largest on record weighed 328 lbs (148 kg). In 1960, a Chinese girl weighing 141 lbs (64 kg) and only 5 ft tall had a cyst removed which weighed 72 lbs (33 kg) which meant that the cyst weighed more than the girl.

One type of cyst, the dermoid variety, contain hair, pieces of bone, scraps of skin, and even teeth. A leading consultant at a London hospital assured the authors that the teeth in dermoid cysts can show up on X-rays. The fluid in dermoid cysts is usually somewhat greasy, while in other types of ovarian cysts it is generally brown or greenish-grey.

Palang

A rod of wood or bone, driven at right-angles through the end of the penis (*qv*). In Borneo, the palang is commonly used to increase stimulation of the vagina. The natives there age quickly and, by the age of 25, are often past their best. Insertion of a palang extends a man's active sexual span.

A man sits in a river until his penis contracts; the coolness of the water also dulls the pain when a nail is bored through the head of the penis, somewhat in the manner of piercing an ear. The palang itself is inserted later. Knobs or points may be attached to each end of the palang; some men even have two palangs.

It is interesting to note that the Borneo Rhinoceros has a natural 'palang' protruding almost two inches each side of its penis when erect.

Penis

The male member, the size and erectness of which can be a cause of great concern. Among the Chinese minorities in the Malay Peninsula it was common to find, especially among the older generation, men who attached lead weights to their penises – which were indeed small and were known locally as 'turtle heads' – since they feared that otherwise their miniscule members would retreat into their bodies.

Conversely, the great grey slug (common in British gardens) has a penis which – when erect – is longer than its body. But the largest penis in the animal world belongs to the Roqual whale whose member can measure 10 ft in length.

Nearer to home, a unique form of revenge was perpetrated by a Pittsburgh woman who, having discovered that her husband was being unfaithful, attached his penis to his thigh with super-glue while he was asleep. The awful consequences were discovered by this unfortunate man when, dreaming of his mistress, he had an involuntary erection . . .

The penis is greatly affected by its circumstances, both emotional and climatic. Nervousness, excess of alcohol, or over-tiredness can make entry into a vagina as difficult as squeezing a marshmallow into a slot machine. Excessive cold, too, has alarming results as discovered by the late David Niven when rehearsing a ski-ing scene for 'The Pink Panther'. Too lightly dressed for the Alpine temperature, he described in his first volume of memoirs, *The Moon's a Balloon* how he 'suddenly got a feeling of absolutely nothing in precisely the spot where I should have been the warmest'. Fearing frostbite, he whizzed down the slope shouting '*Catso gelato!*' and was advised to put it into the snow. Deciding that alcohol would be a better bet, he went to a local bar and 'yelled at the barman to fill a balloon brandy glass with whisky "prontissimo".'

In the lavatory . . . I faced the agony of the thaw and prised out of my ski pants a pale blue acorn. Into the whisky it went and the pain was excruciating. This moment was chosen by a smart Milanese nobleman whom I happened to know to enter with a view to relieving himself. He took in the tableau at a glance.

'David,' he asked in a horrified voice, 'what *are* you doing?'

'I am pissing in a brandyglass,' I muttered between clenched teeth, 'I always do.'

Perspiration

There are about two and a half million sweat glands on the human body which exude over a litre (two pints) of perspiration per day. 'Body odour' is caused by decomposed sweat from the apocrine sweat-glands under the arms. If excessive malodorous sweating cannot be controlled by washing (a simple solution all too rarely used by travellers on London's underground system) or deodorants, a more drastic solution the surgical removal of a patch of skin from the armpit.

Studies made by the US Marine Corps in the Mojave Desert show that three pints of sweat *per hour* are lost walking at 3½ mph in 110 degrees of heat. To function well in desert conditions, no less than three gallons of water must be drunk per day by each man.

Pet Preservation

The rather gruesome habit of handing over one's pet to the taxidermist has now been superceded, for those who have the cash, by freeze-drying. Naturally, this practice originates in California, where your pet is shampooed, gutted, treated with insecticide, filled with embalming fluid and arranged in a suitable pose.

It is then freeze-dried, a process which can take up to nine months for large animals, at a cost of several hundred or even a thousand dollars. When the process is complete the pet is then restored to its favourite place in the owner's house.

Taxidermists are outraged, aesthetically and financially. A leading Californian taxidermist comments: 'You wouldn't stick old grandma in the corner by the hearth just because it makes you feel better. You should also have a little respect for your pet.'

Pharaoh's Ants

Like cockroaches (*qv*) Pharaoh's Ants are common in hospitals where they are extremely destructive. The British Pest Control Association announced in a recent report that these insects are particularly dangerous because they chew their way through plastic, rubber and paper, and can infect sterile dressings and equipment. They have even been found feeding under wound dressings on post-operative patients.

Piercing

Many men as well as women now have their ears pierced, often with several holes in each ear. Less common is nose piercing but other, less visible, parts of the body are sometimes pierced too.

Genesis P. Orridge is leader of a cult based in London which practices a form of witch-craft with sexual intercourse as a vital part of its ritual. He and other members of the cult have their nipples pierced even have rings through the penis. Orridge claims that more pleasure than discomfort is derived from this practice.

Tribes in Africa, the Far East and South America have the custom of distending the earlobes with, perhaps, two dozen heavy rings which dangle to shoulder level. Plugs of wood or bones are sometimes inserted into the huge holes, and the lower lip can be distended in much the same way.

An as-yet unpublished novel which earned world record advances from enthusiastic publishers features a heroine who has diamonds inserted in her labia. What effect this strangely intimate article of jewellery has on her lovers' members must remain a matter of speculation until the book is published.

Piles

More elegantly known as haemorrhoids, piles are inflamed varicose veins (*qv*) at the lower end of the bowel. There are two types: external and internal. The external variety are found outside the bowel in what might be described as the 'anal ante-chamber' and are covered by a thin skin which is either brown or dusky-purple. Internal piles are just inside the anal vent and are covered by mucus membrane. Either crimson or cherry-coloured, they are popularly known among doctors and medical students as 'cherry-bum'.

Most middle-aged people, particularly men who have sedentary jobs, suffer from piles. They are also caused by over-eating and constipation. During a bowel movement, piles cause a sharp burning pain; very protruberant external piles become highly sensitive, even painful, from rubbing against the thighs and clothing. Apart from the pain, great inconvenience is caused by the piles exuding a thin, blood-stained discharge, sometimes called 'a case of leaking bum'. Such external piles sometimes cure themselves by becoming so distended and inflamed that they suppurate and eventually dry up; others become choked off with a blood clot and shrivel into hard little knots which eventually drop off.

Internal piles are less manifest and are usually not painful; however, they can lead to the loss of several ounces of dark blood during a bowel movement and – even more embarrassing – they emit a continuous discharge of mucus mixed with blood which leaves tell-tale marks on clothes, bed-linen and seat-covers.

Internal piles, which doctors advise should be pressed back inside the anus with the fingers after each bowel movement, can be strangled by a ligature or clamp, or cauterised. If their growth is extended, surrounding the whole bowel, they have to be surgically cut away in their entirety, including the rim of mucus membrane lining the bowel. An alternative non-surgical method of treatment is the manual widening of the anus.

Although the surgical operation to remove piles is relatively safe and simple, it occasionally has unexpected hazards. A distinguished London surgeon some time ago performed this operation on an elderly, well-fed French lady. As she lay face-down on the operating table, he bent over her massive raised

preparing to cauterize the freshly-sutured
... At that moment she released a powerful fart
...ich ignited and burnt off his eyebrows.

Placenta

This thick 'cake' of spongy tissue, weighing about 1 ½
pounds, is expelled from the mother's body after
birth, having nourished the foetus during gestation. It
has recently become fashionable not only to invite
friends to be present at the birth of a child but also to
join in eating the placenta. Recipes vary: sometimes it
is fried with butter and onions, sometimes stewed.

Some new mothers prefer to keep the whole
placenta for themselves since they find it dispels post-
natal depression and improves their general health.
One such mother is quoted as saying 'Every time I felt
weepy, I ate a chunk of placenta'. She kept hers in the
refrigerator, preferring it raw because it turned black
when cooked.

Such are the virtues of placenta that it is now used
in an increasing number of beauty aids including
shampoo. Whether human placentas are used, or
whether those in search of beauty smear cow's after-
birth over their faces or massage their heads with pig's
placenta to give their hair more body is not divulged
on the manufacturers' labels.

It also has horticultural uses: midwives have

discovered that roses thrive on placenta, and th.
childbirth expert Sheila Kitzinger buried the placenta
of each of her five children and planted trees on top.

Plague

Also known as the 'Black Death', bubonic plague
ravaged Britain and Europe at least twice. During the
Great Plague of 1664-65, 70,000 people died in
London alone out of a total population of 460,000.
The disease is spread primarily by fleas carried in the
fur of rats (*qv*). The plague bacillus (*Yersinia pestis*) is
so hardy that live specimens were discovered in the
roots of hair still clinging to skulls found in a recently-
excavated plague pit in the foundations of St Bride's
Church, London.

Symptoms include swollen glands known as
'buboes', in the groin and armpits, which can swell
up into black gangrenous ulcers – hence the name
'Black Death'. Infection spread so fast during the
Great Plague that sometimes the drivers of the 'dead
carts' themselves died before reaching the burial
ground. In *The Journal of the Plague Year*, Daniel Defoe
wrote:-

> The work of removing the dead bodies by carts
> was now grown so very odious and dangerous
> that it was complained of that the bearers did not
> take care to clear such houses where all the in-

...ts were dead, but that sometimes the
...es lay several days unburied, till the neigh-
...ouring families were offended with the stench,
and consequently infected.

The pain and fever caused delirium, often with dire
consequences:

This running of distempered people about the
streets was very dismal and the magistrates did
their utmost to prevent it . . . because, as they were
all grievously infected, to be sure, when they were
come to that height, so they were more than ordin-
arily infectious, and it was one of the most dangerous things that could be to touch them. On the
other hand, they generally ran on, not knowing
what they did, till they dropped down stark dead.

In a happier instance, a man dived into the Thames,
swam to the other side and back again, then returned
to his home and bed, to discover:

. . . that this terrible experiment cured him of the
plague, that is to say, that the violent motion of
his arms and legs stretched the parts where the
swellings he had upon him were . . . under his
arms and his groin . . . and caused them to ripen
and break; and that the cold of the water abated
the fever in his blood.

The plague is not confined to the past. Up to six
thousand cases are still reported annually throughout
the world, mostly in South-East Asia, South America
and Southern Africa, but – owing to advances in
medical treatment – only about two hundred of these
die. The last recorded case in Britain was a Suffolk
farmer's wife who caught plague in 1910. She
survived, only to die in the influenza epidemic of
1919.

A curious fact about bubonic plague is that Europeans and others of Caucasian origin are now virtual immune to the disease, and those who do get it suffer only a mild form. A US Army doctor in Saigon told one of the authors that the inoculation against bubonic plague often produced more severe symptoms in Europeans than the disease itself. Black troops in Vietnam, however, were advised to be inoculated if travelling in parts of the country where plague had broken out.

A well-known foreign correspondent from a British daily newspaper insisted on being inoculated on arrival in Saigon and was dangerously ill for four days afterwards; he confessed later that his sexual activity was seriously impaired for three months owing to groin complications.

During a helicopter ride in Vietnam, the author found himself seated next to a Vietnamese army officer who was obviously in bad shape, sweating, vomiting and delirious. When asked if he was wounded, the man whispered, 'J'ai la peste' (I have the plague). The author was unable to change seats and was forced to remain in close proximity for the rest of the flight.

Plaque

'A little white matter which is as thick as if 'twere batter' was Anthony van Leeuwenhoek's description

113

in 1683. Five million cocci are present in milligramme of plaque. How many would have found in the mouth of the old man whom van Leeuwenhoek encountered whose teeth 'were all coated over' and had never been cleaned?

'An unbelievably great company of living animalcules a-swimming more nimbly than any I have ever seen' were observed through van Leeuwenhoek's microscope on this occasion, three hundred years ahead of modern dental hygenists with their ultrasonic scalers emitting bat-like squeaks, and their stern lectures on the use of dental floss.

Psoriasis

A recurring skin disease causing eruptions of small pimples which become reddened crusts, covered with silvery scales. Psoriasis – apart from being painful – is extremely unsightly especially when it attacks the hands, face and head. In the hair, it leaves a trail resembling miniature cornflakes.

In the past, a paste made from sheep's faeces was used to relieve the symptoms but for some reason this is no longer in favour.

Pubic Hair

Among the many fashion crazes of the 'sixties was the well-publicised habit of shaving the pubic hair into unusual shapes. When Mary Quant, the fashion designer, announced to the press that her pubic hair was heart-shaped, John Lennon retaliated that he had shaved his into the shape of a boot.

Less palatable was the discovery of a tobacco tin containing clumps of pubic hair from the bodies of four victims of the Christie murders. Francis Camps' excellent book on the case contains a close-up photograph of the tin and its contents with the comment that the clumps 'show obvious arrangement'.

A famous Parisian 'poule de luxe' in the 1890s attracted her clientele with her abundant pubic hair which 'hung down to her knees', while a Chinese treatise warned against women 'if the pubic hair is coarse and stiff, like bristles, or if it sprouts wildly and in different directions.'

Purgatives

It is not often that a purgative is the subject of a best-selling book but this has happened with *The F-Plan Diet* advocating the benefits of bran. Taken to stimulate the action of the bowels, other purgatives honey, and the less appetising liquid senna pods. Violent purgatives such as , jalap or croton oil can have alarming

merican exchange student at King's College, ridge, told one of the authors that his father had the original for the character of 'Guy Masterson' Damon Runyon's *Guys and Dolls*. At one time uring his career, 'Masterson' became the lover of a glamorous peroxide blonde who had been set up by the gangster Legs Diamond in a penthouse apartment on Chicago's Lake Side. When Legs found out about this illicit affair, he ordered the girl to tell 'Masterson' where to get off. This she did in no uncertain terms, inviting him up to her apartment which was entirely decorated in white to match her own skin-tight white satin dresses and her long-haired white Pekinese dog.

She gave 'Masterson' a drink laced with a powerful purgative, telling him sweetly that he must drink it fast and leave because Legs was due to show up at any moment. 'Masterson' only just made it to the elevator before his bowels exploded in foul profusion – not, however, before he had guessed the cause. So he decided to take his revenge by pretending to ignore the hint and turning up the next evening at the girl's apartment as though nothing had happened.

She seemed surprised to see him so soon and gave him another cocktail which he guessed, correctly, to contain the same ingredients as before. But this time, he refused to be hurried out: he waited until his well-primed bowels began to churn and expand, then calmly took down his trousers and excreted copiously on each of the white armchairs and chesterfield sofas, then picked up the white Pekinese dog, wiped his arse with it, flung it into the arms of his gaping mistress, pulled his trousers on, and walked out of the apartment.

This is believed to be the origin of the slang phrase 'giving someone the bum's rush'.

Rats

In 1960, one of the authors wrote an extended feature on the private life of the common black rat or *Rattus rattus* for the *Manchester Guardian* in which he described how, during sexual intercourse, 'the female's vagina emits a thick, waxy secretion which begins to harden by the time the male withdraws, forming a nearly solid plug which prevents the fresh semen from leaking out and so increases the chances of conception'. This was deleted by the sub-editors.

More than ten million rats live beneath London, many of them in the Westminster area. An attempt by Westminster Council in the 1970s to get rid of them by laying over three thousand poisoned baits simply resulted in a new breed of 'super-rat' which seems impervious to all known poisons. A new way of controlling *Rattus norvegicus*, or brown rat, which arrived in London from Russia in the eighteenth century, is the use of supersonic sound which makes the rats rush around throwing themselves at the sewer walls until they die.

A black rat was recently discovered on board a Boeing 747. It cost £450 to fumigate the plane; but this is a fraction of the cost of damage caused by rats and mice in the UK each year, which runs to £60,000,000 while in the United States the cost totals over $900,000,000.

Rodents have notoriously weak bladders and dribble when they move around, contaminating food and water with their urine (see Weil's Disease).

Rats are not always regarded as vermin and many people insist they make excellent pets. Firemen recently summoned to a blaze in Toledo, Ohio, discovered its bizarre cause: Yentl, a pet rat, was suffering from pneumonia so its owner had taken it into her bed and switched on the electric over-blanket. Snuggled between her breasts, Yentl had chewed through the wires while her owner slept, causing a short-circuit. However, the rat then redeemed itself by licking its owner's face until she woke; Yentl was rewarded with a steak dinner.

In many parts of the Far East, rats are regarded as a culinary delicacy. Nearer to home, within living memory, rat pie has traditionally been served at village festivities in Sussex; and in 1979 a Wisconsin restaurant was fined $50 for serving barbequed rat. Only three of the customers complained – because it was taken off the menu.

Rejuvenation

The elixir of life, secret of eternal youth, has always seemed beyond reach; yet, in the 1950s, Dr Paul Niehans had it in his grasp – or, at any rate, he grasped a considerable amount of his patients' money.

He discovered that, by injecting humans with the glands of certain animals, he could at least restore their energies if not their looks. Among his patients was W. Somerset Maugham who lived to the age of 91, although towards the end of his life he resembled a large unfriendly lizard.

Noël Coward commented on Niehans: 'I believe he injects a horrifying solvent made from an unborn ewe. To judge from the effect on some of my friends, it's a very non-U ewe.' However, Coward himself succumbed to the temptation of the Niehans treatment and, as he told one of the authors: 'I know I look terribly, terribly old but I feel terribly, terribly young,' after he had been injected with monkey glands. The fact that Coward in his last years bore an alarming resemblance to a pickled monkey may have been coincidental.

Round-worm

Also known as the maw-worm, this parasite causes the tropical disease Ascariasis which can cause obstruction of the gut. The worms resemble undulating spaghetti; the female is nine inches long, the male two inches shorter. Round-worms flourish in unhygenic conditions and their eggs are often accidentally eaten by children playing in dirt and then putting their fingers in their mouths. The eggs then develop inside the intestines.

Although round-worms are usually excreted, one of the authors was the unfortunate witness of a fellow-journalist who had picked up round-worm from eating tropical fruit and who, vomiting after an excess of palm wine, realised that his chunder was writhing on the floor.

Saliva

Kisses on and off screen have become less passionate with the AIDS scare; perhaps they would stop altogether if everyone realised that saliva contains ten million or more bacteria per cubic centimetre. Seen under a microscope, it also carries numerous 'epithelial scales' which Theodor Rosebury describes in his brilliant book *Life on Man* as resembling 'wet dandruff'.

Scaldrum Dodge

The nineteenth-century philanthropist Henry Mayhew observed that, among the many genuine cases of need he found in his huge survey of poverty, *London Labour and the London Poor*, were a number of beggars exhibiting simulated sores. He wrote:

A few had lacerated their flesh in reality; but the majority had resorted to the less painful operation known as the 'Scaldrum Dodge'. This consists in covering a portion of the leg or arm with soap to the thickness of a plaister, and then saturating the whole with vinegar. The vinegar causes the soap to blister and assume a festering appearance, and thus the passer-by is led to believe that the beggar is suffering from a real sore. The 'Scaldrum Dodge' came in with penny postage, daguerro-types and other modern innovations. In less scientific period it was wholly unknown; and sores were produced by burns and lacerations which the mendicants inflicted upon themselves with a ruthless hand. An old man informed me that he had known a man prick the flesh of his leg all over, in order to produce blood and give the appearance of an ulcerous disease.

Scalping

Widely practised in the past by many – though not all

D.O.D.F.—7

– North American Indian tribes. The scalp of an enemy was not only a war trophy but was also supposed to transfer his power to the scalp-taker.

A circular cut was made round the head; then the victor sank his teeth into the hair and skin, and the scalp was torn off. Scalping did not always result in death, though life afterwards cannot have been comfortable.

Among the many murders which take place in the United States, a recent case stands out for its originality. The victim, a young girl, was scalped by her murderer who wore her long-haired scalp as well as her clothes in order to escape over the Canadian border.

Self-immolation

A religious practice which gained world-wide notoriety in the early Sixties, when Buddhist monks in South-East Asia took to pouring cans of petrol over themselves in public places, protesting against the Vietnam war. A spate of such acts occurred in 1963 after the beautiful Madame Nhu, sister of South Vietnam's Premier Ngo Diem, had inflamed the Buddhist community by referring to these martyrs as 'barbecqued *bonzes*' (Buddhist monks). This culminated in Ngo Diem's murder.

In 1966 a further spate of self-immolations took

place in Hue and Saigon; many *bonzes* and rebellious students set themselves alight, this time with the world's television networks at hand. One of the authors witnessed an incident outside a Saigon pagoda. A distinguished American television journalist, anxious to catch his midday transmission deadline, approached an elderly monk sitting in his saffron robes on a pile of wood, a four-gallon can of petrol clutched in his arms. The journalist interrupted the old man's prayers, asking: 'Excuse me, Venerable, but is there any chance that you will immolate yourself before twelve noon?'

Semen

A milky fluid ejaculated at the time of orgasm and containing approximately 100,000,000 spermatozoa (*qv*) per millilitre. Perhaps it is surprising to realise that only two to four millilitres (less than a teaspoonful) of semen is usually ejaculated with each orgasm, though amounts of up to fifteen millilitres have been recorded. If ejaculation occurs in a restricted space (such as the vagina) the distance semen travels is only six to nine inches but distances of more than three feet are possible in less confined conditions.

The indefatigable Tom Dribert (See Diarrhoea) noted that poverty – especially poor diet – produces thin, weak semen and that one of his young lovers, rather than producing a stain on the sheet recalling the map of Ireland, emitted a 'puny leakage' resembling nothing more than the Isle of Wight.

Staying in a grand country house, the son of a well-known peer of the realm had a wet dream and left a large stain – he was obviously well-nourished – on the crisp white linen sheet. Before he left the next morning, he drew a circle round the stain and wrote 'SORRY!'.

See also Oral Sex.

Sewage

The sewers of London have for nearly eight centuries provided a source of undiluted filth. Several times, the bowels of London have been constipated, leading to explosions of sewage under the streets followed by epidemics and widespread deaths, including some from drowning. In Medieval times it was common for citizens to perish after falling into cess-pools built behind or under their houses. In 1326 a sewage worker or 'gong fermor' called Richard the Raker is recorded as having 'drowned monstruously in his own excrement'. Death through suffocation was also frequent.

In 1328 there was a complaint to the Assizes of Nuisance by one William Sprot that his neighbours,

Adam and William Mere, had allowed their 'cloaca' to overflow their party wall into his house.

The Elizabethan poet Sir John Harington invented a 'water closet' driven, to do so, perhaps, by finding: Even in the goodliest and stateliest palaces of this realm this same whorson sawcie stink . . . great and well-contrived houses have vaults and secret passages under ground to convey away both the ordure and other noisome things. What with fish-water coming from the kitchens, bloud and garbage of foul, washing of dishes, and the excrement of other houses joyned together, and all these in moyst weather stirred a little with some small streams of rain water. For, as the proverb is,

'Tis noted as the nature of a sinke,

Ever the more 'tis stird, the more to stink.

However, there was no great enthusiasm during the reign of Queen Elizabeth I to replace cess-pits with Harington's water-closet. It was found that the nitrogen from excrement could be used to manufacture saltpetre, the main ingredient of gunpowder. Indeed, it can be said that the great Elizabethan age was made possible largely by harnessing the power of London's shit, for use in the cannons of privateers against the fleets of Spain. Gangs of saltpetremen were hired by the Queen to roam through the city and break into private houses where they would dig up the floors of rooms, regardless of their occupants even if in childbirth or dying, in search of cesspits.

By 1633 the demands of decency began to be translated into law and the Statute of the Streets made it illegal to 'widraw' – i.e. defecate – in public. The penalty was £1 at a time when the average yearly income of a common labourer was £7, but this did not prevent house-holders from emptying chamber-pots out of upper windows, accompanied by the warning 'gardy loo' (gardez l'eau = watch out for the water).

Samuel Pepys noted in his diary for 20th October 1660:

> This morning one came to me where to make me a window into my cellar in lieu of one that Sir W. Batten had stopped up; and going down into my cellar to look, I put my foot into a great heap of turds, by which I find Mr Turner's house of office is full and comes into my cellar, which doth trouble me.

In the nineteenth century, a vast network of brick-built sewers was constructed under most of London. Their contents flowed untreated into the Thames which itself became a vast, putrid, disease-ridden sewer flowing sluggishly into the sea. Then, in 1859, came the Great Stink – an appalling fog of fumes which was so overwhelming that the windows of the House of Commons had to be draped with curtains soaked in chloride of lime. According to a contemporary account, the roofs of the sewer galleries were hung with congealed putrescence, like stalactites, up to three feet in length. These sewers also contained thousands of dead dogs, cats, rats, and offal from the slaughter-houses.

This state of affairs was not confined to London. Queen Victoria, while being shown round Trinity College, Cambridge, asked the Master, 'What are all those pieces of paper floating down the river?' At that time, all the sewage of Cambridge poured directly into the River Cam but – rather than telling the Queen the truth – Dr Whewell, the Master, explained that they were notices explaining that bathing was forbidden.

The Fleet River, one of London's many waterways

now concealed, had long been an open drain before being covered over. Among the sludge it carried to the Thames was the refuse from Lambeth knackers' yards and the slaughter-houses of Whitehall, together with various effluents from tanneries and tar-works on both sides of the river. At the very time when Sydney Smith wrote to Lady Gray in 1834 'I am in better health and drinking nothing but London water', the Thames was described as being a greenish coffee colour, deepening to that of black treacle near the outlets of the sewage tunnels, and covered by a viscous steaming scum where the mud-banks were exposed at low tide.

The Victorian sewer system is now beginning to cave in and rats (*qv*) proliferate. How long before London suffers another Great Stink?

Sex Aids

False penises or 'dildoes' in various forms, ranging from carrots or candles to the latest in battery-operated vibrators, have been used since the days of ancient Babylon. Perhaps today's best-known false penis belongs to Sir Les Patterson, the Australian Cultural Attache and author of that invaluable book *The Traveller's Tool*, otherwise known as Barry Humphries. On a recent trip to Dubai, Sir Les had his 'tool' confiscated by puzzled customs officers and had to give his performance without this vital piece of equipment.

The New York newspaper *Village Voice* has proclaimed 'the new lesbian sexual culture' (haven't they heard of Sappho?) and quotes an example of what can happen when two sexual minorities meet.

One pioneering lesbian ordered a custom-made lower body harness for her strap-on dildo, and the nice 'gay toymaker' at the leather store graciously took the measurements. But when she got her new scxual apparatus home, she couldn't figure out how to wear it correctly. Embarrassed but undaunted, she returned to the store for technical assistance.

'You're wearing it backwards,' said her leather specialist.

'Backwards?' she said, astonished. 'But then how do you get the dildo in the front?'

'In the *front*?' he blushed. 'I made it to fit a butt plug.'

(See also Masturbation and Palang)

Sexual Intercourse

The authors assume that readers of this book know at least the rudiments of sexual intercourse, unlike the young couple in the Cotswolds who – it was recently reported – could not understand their failure to produce a baby; it turned out that they did not know the facts of life which were then kindly explained to them by the local vet.

It is commonly thought that rabbits perform sexual intercourse more frequently than humans but a 1985 study by Professor Dennis Lincoln of Edinburgh shows that humans are ten thousand times more sexually active than rabbits. In Britain each year, 1,000,000,000 acts of sexual intercourse are performed, resulting in three million litres of semen (*qv*) being ejaculated, at a conservative estimate.

Shrunken Heads

Many tribes have taken trophies from their enemies' bodies (see Castration and Scalping) and head-hunting was practised until recently in Borneo. However, certain South American tribes, not content with possessing the heads of their enemies, shrink them.

First the skin is removed from the skull and boiled, then hot stones and·sand are used to shrink it. The skin is moulded to keep the shape of the face; slivers of wood are used to hold the lips together.

Other tribes shrink the whole body, while the Mundurucu of Brazil dry their enemies' heads, stuff them, and carry them on sticks. In Borneo, skulls are hung in nets from the ceiling of huts.

Smegma

A pungent, off-white waxy substance reminiscent in texture and odour of over-ripe cheese. Smegma accumulates under the foreskin causing irritation if the penis is not frequently and thoroughly washed. It is a combination of decomposing skin cells and genital secretions, and is a rich breeding-ground for bacteria.

Ambergris, long valued for its medicinal properties and now used as a fixative for scent, is in fact the smegma of the sperm whale.

Distinguished author Brian Aldiss, in his novel *The Eighty-minute Hour* described a 'monster slobby yellow cheese' which 'tasted as if it had been whipped together from rhinocerus smegma.'

Snakes

Since antiquity, snakes have aroused fear and revulsion. This ancient terror has given rise to many myths and superstitions about snakes, one of which is that the mamba attacks on sight and can move as fast as a horse. In fact, although their speed is phenomenal, they rarely attack without provocation, though, once wounded, they will retaliate.

On the coast road of Mozambique, from Maputo to Beira, one of the authors saw a squashed snake – and sometimes a live one – about every hundred yards. The car windows had to be kept closed despite the heat, in case an injured mamba rose up and struck one of the passengers. At every petrol station the attendant checked the car in case a snake had wrapped itself round the axle.

A Norwegian sailor once went ashore in Singapore, got very drunk, and passed out in the gutter. In the early hours of the morning a large python, sensing something warm and meaty, opened its jaws over the sailor's left foot and started swallowing. This it did with such finesse that its hundred teeth did not even scratch the skin; the man's drunken sleep was so heavy that he woke only when the snake's jaws reached his groin and jammed. By the time help came, the python's powerful digestive juices had already started to disintegrate the sailor's boot, trouser and leg. The snake had to be slit open to release the sailor, and only swift amputation of the leg at the local hospital saved his life.

In 1950 a young secretary working for the Malayan High Commission in Kuala Lumpur was served an exotic soup in a Chinese restaurant. Soon afterwards, she complained of violent stomach pains. No cause could be found; the pains increased, her stomach began to swell. Her intestinal tract became blocked and she began to suffer serious loss of weight. Only after a detailed X-ray of her stomach was it discovered, several weeks after the first pains, that she had a fully-grown cobra in her stomach. She had eaten a cobra's egg in the soup, it had hatched, and every four to six weeks – the normal intervals between feeds – it had helped itself to the contents of her stomach by eating into her intestines.

Snot

A slimy secretion of mucus from the nose which contains a number of substances such as dead cells cast off from the surface of the nasal membranes, acid deposits, and particles of dust and dirt trapped in the nasal hairs. Accumulations of snot, known generally as bogeys, vary in colour from lettuce-green – usually the more fluid variety – to those of a more rubbery consistency which tend to battleship-grey. Occasionally, more granular bogeys resembling cake crumbs emerge. One of the few consolations in the wake of a heavy head cold is the pleasure of scraping these deposits off the walls of the nasal passage, preferably with a longish finger-nail.

Perhaps it is the peculiarly cloying, solid texture of bogeys rather than their slightly salty though barely discernible taste that seems to arouse in so many of us – and not merely children – an atavistic urge to excavate and then consume them with relish (see also Nose-picking).

Consumption of snot is not confined to children. It can lead to a rare but by no means unknown sexual perversion. A certain London society beauty in the 1930s had a dismaying experience when she was invited by a seemingly respectable man-about-town for tea at his bachelor chambers in Mayfair. He had given his maid the afternoon off and prepared the delicate sandwiches himself. They contained cucumber and a slimy grey paste resembling crushed oysters. When the lady asked him what this was, he replied brutally: 'Snot, my dear.' He then asked if he could eat some of hers. She made her excuses and left.

Sootikin or Sutikin

A small, mouse-shaped deposit formed in the vaginal cleft, usually of poorer women who did not wear undergarments – common until the nineteenth century. A sootikin built up over several weeks, even months, of not washing. It was composed of particles of soot, dirt, sweat, smegma (*qv*) and vaginal and menstrual discharge. When it reached a certain size and weight, it tended to work loose and drop from under the woman's skirt.

Contemporary writings, including those of Pepys and Boswell, mention men employed in London churches to sweep up sootikins after services. There even exists one scurrilous account, from an anonymous source, of a tell-tale sootikin being allegedly found under – or suspiciously close to – Queen Anne's chair in St Paul's Cathedral during the Thanksgiving Service for the end of the War of the Spanish Succession.

Spermatozoa

Although men have been producing sperm since the Creation, it was not discovered until the mid-nineteenth century that these minute, tadpole-like organisms, were vital for conception.

The Dutch pioneer in microscopy, Anthony van Leeuwenhoek, first observed sperm. In 1677 he described them to the Royal Society in London as a great quantity of 'animalcules' resembling 'river eels'. It was thought at the time that sperm were some kind of parasite living in the semen (*qv*).

Each ejaculation of semen carries between 200 million and 400 million spermatozoa, though this usually decreases with age. However, Havelock Ellis, the pioneer sexologist, noted a man aged 103 who still produced live sperm.

Spitting

Like nose-picking (*qv*), spitting in public is a disgusting habit, though unlike the former, it seems to be on the decrease – no longer do we provide brass spittoons in public places.

Charles Dickens, on a visit to America in 1842, was fascinated and appalled by the American habit of chewing tobacco and spitting copiously and referred to it frequently in his *American Notes*. In a letter to John Forster he describes the 'gentleman's car' on an American railroad train:

> The flashes of saliva flew so perpetually and incessantly out of the windows all the way, that it looked as though they were ripping open feather-beds inside and letting the wind dispose of the feathers. But this spitting is universal . . . I have twice seen gentlemen, at evening parties in New York, turn aside when they were not engaged in conversation, and spit upon the drawing-room carpet. And in every bar-room and hotel passage the stone floor looks as if it were paved with open oysters – from the quantity of this kind of deposit which tesselates it all over . . .

Strangulated Hernia

Over-strenuous exercise, severe constipation, or even a habitual cough may cause a rupture in the abdominal wall through which part of the intestines (*qv*) may protrude. Strangulation of the hernia occurs when the blood circulating through the intestines is cut off by the sides of the gap through which it is protruding. This can easily become gangrenous and lead to a rapid death.

Perhaps Mr Peter Dowdeswell of Northamptonshire did not realise this when, against doctor's orders, he took part in a snail-eating contest despite a strangulated hernia. However, he managed to eat only 196 snails in 2 minutes 43.95 seconds while Mr Thomas 'Muskrat' Greene of Maryland broke the world snail-eating record by consuming 220 snails, weighing one kilo (2.2 lbs), in the time. Mr Dowdeswell commented: 'I thought I was going to throw up. I was in pain right from the start.'

Syphilis

Although a mild form of syphilis was known in ancient Rome, a far more severe variety raged through Europe in the late fifteenth century. Cortez, while exploring South America, ordered his men not to commit bestiality (*qv*) with llamas, but was unable to prevent a virulent form of the disease from being transmitted in this way to his troops.

Columbus, too, unwittingly brought back the disease from his New World explorations and it quickly spread through Spain, Italy and France. When Charles VIII of France attempted to take the Kingdom of Naples, so virulent was the disease among both the invading and defending armies that neither side won. Charles had to return to France but his troops continued to infect their camp followers (known as 'bagages') and other women throughout the homeward journey.

The disease was spread to Scotland by mercenary soldiers. In 1498, the burghers of Aberdeen made a law that ordered 'all light women to desist from their vice and sin of venery' in the vain hope that this would curtail its spread.

Symptoms include skin ulcers, known as 'buboes'; sores resembling snail trails in the mouth and on the genitals; and infectious swellings in the bones, with the palate and nose being gradually eaten away. The only known cure at the time was mercury (*qv*) which itself made the hair and teeth fall out. A rash of spots and pustules spreads over the upper body and head with, frequently, a band of spots across the brow which eighteenth-century doctors called the 'crown of Venus'. In the 1890s, Professor Brøck of Oslo was the first to realise that the traditional mercury treatment was useless, and he made a detailed study of the disease. Brøck observed the final stages: tumours known as 'gummas' which eat away skin and flesh, boring painfully into the bone; damage to the heart, causing rupture of the aorta; affliction of the brain, causing delusions. Autopsies have shown that the brain shrinks when attacked by syphilis.

Nor is the brain all that shrinks, for the penis can deteriorate alarmingly. One of Britain's most eminent venereal specialists – the former chief 'clap' doctor of the Royal Navy, now happily working for the National Health Service – records that some years ago he was contacted by a friend who had woken one morning to find his penis resembling a cold burnt

137

sausage. Other symptoms, including fever and rash, pointed to the secondary stage of syphilis. Anti-biotics only seemed to exacerbate the affliction until the wretched man was confined to his bed with his member encased in a weird 'Heath Robinson' device: a sheath of plaster of Paris between bat-like wings to facilitate drainage of pus and other odious matter, while the head of his penis was capped by a rubber snout and tube so that he could urinate into a bottle.

The eminent doctor was not only trying to cure his friend but was also entrusted with the delicate job of tracking down all his patient's recent partners – both real and alleged – since the man in question was a heavy drinker and could not always remember whether or not he had performed satisfactorily. The ladies in question were far from pleased with these investigations.

Eventually, the 'disease' turned out to be a false alarm, having been caused by an allergic reaction to anti-biotics and painkillers which the patient had been taking following an operation for piles (*qv*).

For a graphic description of syphilis, the following passage from *Mars in Capricorn* by Beverley Cross cannot be bettered:

He sprawled in the passage and his fat yellow stomach stuck out from between his greasy shirt and the unbuttoned top of his jeans. Below his navel the horrid skin was a wet mess of pustules and a cockroach crawled across his belly exploring the angry sore.

Between us, we tore away the trousers and examined the livid rash which spread from his navel to his thigh. 'Do you know what this is? asked the mate.

'Sweat-rash,' I ventured. The mate shook his

138

head. 'No, lad,' he said. 'This is the pox. This is what comes of too many black girls and too much jig-jig.'

Tapeworm

A parasite which feeds on the contents of its host's intestines. The tapeworm is transferred to humans in under-cooked meat, especially pork. Anchored to the bowel wall by the suckers and tiny hooks on its pin-sized, yellowish head, the flat white body extends through the intestines absorbing digested food through its entire surface. Tapeworms often reach a length of forty feet – some ten feet longer than the average human intestine – and cause great discomfort in the abdomen.

The film director John Irvin recalls an incident on location in North Yemen when an unfortunate Arab technician was afflicted by tapeworm so badly that life became unbearable. His trousers were lowered and he was laid over the bonnet of a Land Rover while the tapeworm was coaxed out of his anus with the promise of a saucer of curdled milk. When the tiny head finally made its appearance, attaching its suckers to the saucer, another technician expertly wound the body round a pencil which he began to turn gently, drawing out the worm as though reeling in a fishing line. The operation took several hours since any violent motion would have snapped off the body which could then have recoiled inside the rectum and produced another head.

Irvin states that, when the job had been successfully completed, the body had been delicately winched around two pencils, both filled to overflowing, and that the worm was at least as long as a cricket pitch.

Tattooing

For at least four thousand years tattooing has been used as a permanent body decoration. It often has religious or tribal significance, including the latter-day 'tribes' of Hell's Angels and punks. The methods remain very much the same as in ancient times: pigments such as cinnabar (red), cobalt (blue) and carbon (black) are punched deep into the skin with needles. The main hazards are infection from the needles and the fact that tattoos cannot be removed without leaving a scar.

In his splendid book *Into the Heart of Borneo* describing his chaotic journey with the poet James Fenton, Redmond O'Hanlon writes of guide, Dana:

Covered in circles and rossettes, whorls and lines (soot from a cooking pot, mixed with sweetened water, and punched into the skin with a bamboo stick and small hammer) the large tattoo on his throat (the most painful of all to suffer, and the most likely to cause septicaemia) testified to his immediate courage; on his thighs an intricate pattern of stylised Rhinoceros hornbill heads bespoke his chiefly status; and on the top joints of his fingers a series of dots and cross-hatchings suggested that he had taken heads in battle.

To prove that *il faut souffrir pour etre belle*, certain brave women are having lines of black or dark blue tattooed on their eye-lids, to save having to renew their eye-liner every day. Oddest of all was the baby born in April 1985 with a tattoo on its arm dated 1917. An anchor draped with a banner and marked with the name of the ship USS *Cyclops* could also be seen. However, the tattoo faded a few days after the child's birth.

Teratoma Tumour

A rare birth defect, caused by an ovum beginning to separate and form twins, without the separation being completed. One of the embryos does not develop fully and often lodges inside the body of the normal twin. This can result in an otherwise healthy child 'giving birth' to a foetus, usually still-born though – in a few cases – living briefly after its 'birth'.

Not long ago, in a suburb of Paris, a three-year old boy's stomach began to 'protrude like a watermelon'. X-rays showed a foetus in his abdomen and a delicate operation had to be performed quickly because the developing foetus could have caused permanent damage or even death to its 'brother'.

A similar case happened a few years ago in Algeria, and a thirty-year old Finnish man discovered that the cause of his respiratory problems was a six-inch male foetus in his lung.

Testicles

The most vulnerable part of a man's anatomy, contained in a pouch of skin known as the scrotum. Millions of spermatozoa (*qv*) are produced in the testicles each day and leave through a complex system of ducts over twenty feet long.

The culinary delights of testicles have yet to be fully exploited. One of the authors, dining at a small Arab restaurant in Jaffa, saw 'Sheep's Eggs' chalked up on the menu board. A graphic – and accurate – imagination prevented her from ordering this dish.

A rare but increasingly popular delicacy in the United States is bulls' testicles, known more appetizingly as 'Rocky Mountain Oysters'. Nearly 50,000 lb of these are consumed each year in Colorado alone, and recent interest from further afield means that over 150,000 lb are now being produced. The 'Oysters', which are cooked with secret ingredients and accompanied by a special sauce, are being marketed widely by an enterprising Denver businessman who certainly has a lot of balls.

Because of their delicate nature, the testicles are particularly vulnerable to injury and disease. Perhaps the worst affliction is elephantiasis which is prevalent especially in warm climates. The testicles swell to an enormous size and the penis gradually disappears. Curiously, the patient often enjoys otherwise excellent health. In parts of Africa and the Indian sub-continent, it is quite common to see men propelling their gigantic testicles in a wheel-barrow.

A doctor in the French West Indies about a century ago removed from a Creole a tumour caused by elephantiasis which weighed 180 lb, was over 2 ft in diameter and had a circumference of nearly 6 ft. Surgery lasted eight hours and each cut of the knife resulted in a colossal haemorrhage of blood. The operation was successful – but the patient died.

Thrush

A fungal infection like athlete's foot, thrush flourishes mainly in the vagina (*qv*) where the yeast-like substance which causes the infection thrives in damp, warm conditions. At least fifty thousand new cases occur in Britain each year and, since this is a recurring infection, the number of sufferers runs into millions.

Although it can be transferred without sexual

contact, this is often the cause. A dark, strong-smelling, frothy discharge appears, accompanied by a rash on the genitals and a compulsion to urinate, and searing pain when doing so.

Cures for thrush include cottage cheese, yoghurt, cider vinegar, herbs and garlic, all of which can either be consumed or applied – separately or together – to the affected area.

Trans-sexualism

The first sex change operation carried out in the UK was at the appropriately-named Middlesex Hospital, where Robert Cowell – former test-pilot and racing motorist – became Miss Roberta Cowell in the late 1950s. Ten years later, she appeared in the bankruptcy court having spent all the money paid to her by the Sunday newspapers on Bentleys and fur coats.

Perhaps the most notorious trans-sexual is April Ashley, defendant in a famous case brought by her husband, Arthur Corbett, who claimed that he had not realised when he married her that she had been born a man. The former George Jamieson, ex-merchant seaman, insisted that she was female but lost the case. Although a medical witness testified that she had a vagina and was therefore female, Ms Ashley had not been able to divest herself of her male chromosomes. Whatever her sex, April Ashley is now a popular member of London society; her glamorous clothes and smooth-skinned face are greatly admired.

In the American mid-West, a rare case has been reported of identical twins who both wish to change their sex from female to male. This transformation is even more difficult to achieve than the more common male-to-female, and involves raising a flap of skin on the thigh from which a penis is moulded around a plastic tube giving a permanent erection. A major problem is maintaining the blood supply to the end of the penis which all too frequently drops off as a result. However, neither male or female trans-sexuals are capable of orgasm since the genital nerves are inevitably severed by surgery.

A French doctor has recently revealed that, in 1979, she performed a sex change operation on herself (see also Castration). Because she could not persuade any of her colleagues to operate on her since sex changes were illegal in France, she took female sex hormones and then removed her genitalia under a local anaesthetic. Later, she 'attached an artificial vagina' which she had bought in the Netherlands.

Trepanation

Imagine being permanently high without having to take expensive, dangerous drugs. There is just one drawback: this euphoric state of mind is achieved by having a hole drilled in the skull.

Trepanation – also known as trepanning or trephining – was widely practised for many centuries as a cure for madness and other disorders. The Ancient Greeks used trepanation as the cure for all head injuries. In the 17th century, when 'trephining was freely resorted to, even for inveterate migraine', Prince William of Orange is said to have received this treatment seventeen times.

For most of this century, trepanation was out of favour until it was revived in the 1960s by a Dutchman, Bart Huges. His beliefs appealed to the jeunesse dorée of the Swinging Sixties in London, coinciding with the popularity of LSD which Huges also did much to promote. Among his disciples was Joseph Mellen who decided to take the plunge and bore a hole in his own head.

This decision was not followed by immediate success. First, Mellen tried using an instrument specially designed for trepanning, a combined corkscrew and saw. However, he turned out to be remarkably thick-skulled and his first, solo, attempt was a failure. Success evaded him again when, with his friend Amanda Feilding's help, he tried a second time; at the crucial moment he fainted, was carried off to hospital and found himself being observed by a team of amazed psychiatrists.

Third time lucky: Mellen succeeded in removing a disc of bone, causing 'an ominous-sounding schlurp and the sound of bubbling'. But to make sure of complete success, Mellen repeated the operation, this time using an electric drill – which fused. Finally, at the fifth attempt, he drilled at least an inch deep and has felt full of joie de vivre ever since.

Amanda Feilding then decided to trepan herself. Benefitting from Joseph Mellen's experience, she planned her operation carefully, and her first attempt was successful. First, she cut into her head with a scalpel and then calmly bored through her skull with an electric drill.

A film of the operation, made by Joseph Mellen and entitled *Heartbeat in the Brain*, has been shown world-wide, though it does have an alarming effect on audiences who tend to faint when the blood spurts out of Amanda's head and she turns smiling towards the camera.

Urination

Involuntary urination, as we all know, can be instigated by the sound of running water; it can also be prompted by submerging the hand in water. Some years ago, a holiday resort in the South of France was plagued by a lascivious character who used to prowl the beach looking for young women lying asleep in the sun. He then used to dip their fingers carefully into a glass of tepid water and watch them urinate into their swimsuits.

Excess of alcohol has a bad effect on the bladder (see Bed-wetting.) During the Old Vic season in 1953, Richard Burton was playing Henry V. He drank several pints of beer at the Union Jack Club in Waterloo Road during the interval of one packed performance. In the second half, he was taken short during a long speech. Turning his back on the audience, he relieved himself through his chain mail. The urine flowed down into the ancient footlights where it boiled, letting off a steaming cloud of toxic gas. The first ten rows of stalls had to be temporarily evacuated.

After the performance, his suit of chain mail was found to be rusty and had to be sent away to be oiled, at a cost of £40 – which happened to be exactly the amount of the actor's weekly salary at the time. It was duly deducted from his next wage packet by the management.

Urine Therapy

Therapy in every form is extremely popular in California. Magazines such as *Utopian Classroom* – describing itself as 'A Journal of Do-It-Yourself Mental Health' – abound and new therapies are tried as often as new clothes.

Perhaps the least palatable therapy currently favoured is that of drinking or being injected by one's own urine. At least one Los Angeles 'specialist' charges insecure film stars large fees for injecting them with a substance which they have – after all – produced themselves.

One English actress decided to economise and drink her urine mixed with apple juice, something she now does regularly. She also uses it as a facial lotion and for healing cuts. Urine is also good for sunburn and skin disease. However, its use is not entirely new. In his book *Scatalogical Rites of All Nations*, published in 1891, J.G. Bourke wrote that in the seventeenth century: 'One's own urine was drunk as a preservative from the plague . . . (and) as a drink for lues veneris (syphilis)'

And, also in that century, Michael Etmuller wrote: The urine of a boy twelve years old who had been drinking wine was placed in a receptacle, surrounded by horse-dung for forty days, allowed to putrefy, then decanted upon human ordure, and distilled in an alembic. The resulting fluid was looked on as a great 'anodyne' for all sorts of pains, and given both internally and externally, as well as in scurvy, hypochondria, cachexy, yellow and black jaundice, calculi of the kidney and bladder, epilepsy, and mania.

However, the last word must go to the son of that English actress who, when she tried to persuade him to try urine therapy as a cure for his asthma, said he would prefer to have the asthma.

Vagina

The vagina has, perhaps, more uses than the penis. It is a favourite hiding place for smuggling anything from drugs to diamonds; a less obvious use is as a purse. The Victorian author of *My Secret Life* describes inserting shillings into a woman's vagina until eighty-four coins were lodged there, and stayed put even when she walked around the room. It is not known whether the woman in question derived any pleasure from having the coins in her vagina or, even, whether she was allowed to keep them.

Other unusual objects have been found in vaginas. A notorious episode in Shirley Conran's novel *Lace* involves a live goldfish in a vagina but this is not confined to fiction; the authors have it on good authority that a real-life case came to light recently in a London hospital – or perhaps it was a veterinary surgery.

Coca-cola bottles are now rare but the curved lip and rounded top tempted a young girl at a Swiss finishing school some years ago to masturbate (*qv*) with one. A vacuum formed, the bottle was clamped to her vagina, and it had to be surgically removed.

During the Swinging Sixties in London, many drugs raids were carried out by the police. One of these has long been rumoured to have been particularly unusual: it was claimed that Convent-educated Marianne Faithfull was discovered with a Mars Bar in her vagina which her friends, including Mick Jagger, were taking turns to consume.

But perhaps the most unusual case occured when a doctor examined a woman complaining of pains in her lower abdomen. He inserted a speculum and shone a torch up her vagina, to be faced with a strangely familiar sight:

$$1 \quad 3$$
$$2 \quad 4 \quad R$$

It was the gear-stick knob of a Morris Minor.

Vaginismus

A sudden spasm or contraction of the vaginal muscles. If this occurs before penetration, it impedes entry of the penis (*qv*) and can be caused by nervousness or reluctance to have sexual intercourse (*qv*).

Vaginismus can also occur in the final stages of intercourse, making it impossible for the penis to be removed from the vagina. An embarrassing scene occured some years ago at Parker's Piece, a field in Cambridge much favoured by amorous undergraduates. An ambulance had to be called when a rowing blue in his last year at one of Cambridge's smartest colleges was discovered behind a bush with a French *au pair* girl, in circumstances described by the Head Proctor as 'locked in a deadly embrace'.

Varicose Veins

Nearly seventy per cent of adults suffer from varicose veins in their legs, caused by a surfeit of blood dilating the veins. The same condition causes piles (*qv*) and varicocele, or distension of the veins in the testicles, which causes the veins in the spermatic cord to resemble 'a bag of worms'.

As well as being unsightly, varicose veins are painful and, if left untreated, may cause large, hideous ulcers which harden and give off an offensive-smelling discharge.

Although they may be hereditary, varicose veins are exacerbated by long hours of standing still. Barmaids, hairdressers, sentries, shop assistants and waiters are all at risk. Surgeons, too, are prone to varicose veins caused by long and lucrative hours spent at the operating table.

Surgical removal of the offending veins is the ultimate treatment. A small flap of skin is raised on the inside of the patient's thigh and calf, the vein is severed and tied with a reef-knot of catgut or silk at each end, and the swollen portion pulled out.

A millionaire in St Louis, Missouri, once made a bet with some friends that he could string a tennis racquet with discarded varicose veins from the local hospital. He won, although the veins were not supple enough even after prolonged soaking in oil, and his game did not improve.

Vomit

The habit of involuntary vomiting has gained an irresistible fascination in recent times, thanks largely to the work of Barry Humphries, the Australian comedian. His comic strip creation, 'The Adventures of Barrie Mackenzie', in *Private Eye* brought vomiting to the forefront of the public imagination and introduced many synonyms for this activity. Such poetic metaphors as 'Technicolor yawn', 'Park a tiger' and 'cry "Ruth" ' owe their popularity to Humphries who himself enacted an unforgettable real-life drama while on a flight to Australia. Discreetly, he poured a can of mixed vegetable salad into an air-sick bag, then simulated noisy vomiting. Once all the nearby passengers' attention had been attracted, he started eating the contents of the bag.

There are occasions when this disgusting natural function obtains a graphic, almost cosmic, glory all of its own. One of the authors recalls an incident at Coney Island, the gigantic fairground outside New York. A distinguished friend of his, a member of a leading East Coast family and at the time a top New York publisher, took him there while suffering from a bad hangover, he made the mistake of stopping for a greasy hamburger, washed down by several beers. They then went for a ride on the huge Ferris wheel, during which the individual cars went spinning round at a vertiginous speed. Hurtling through the air upside-down at the apex of the wheel, he was violently sick. The wheel could not be stopped and, for several minutes, the vomiter, his discharge, and his fellow passengers spun on. The vomit continued to circulate by centrifugal force but, as its density was gradually dispersed in the air so its speed declined, until it was spread out in a thin spray evenly dispersed in a vast circular pattern, coating every passenger on the wheel. It was noted afterwards that the only person who emerged unscathed was the vomiter himself.

Water

Far from being pure, tap water, even now in the big cities of Europe and the United States, contains many impurities. However, things have improved. In the eighteenth century, Tobias Smollett wrote:

If I drink water I must quaff the mawkish contents of an open aqueduct, exposed to all manner of defilement, or swallow what comes from the River Thames . . . human excrement is the least offensive part of the concrete which is composed of all the drugs, minerals and poisons used in mechanics and manufacture enriched with the putrifying carcases of beasts and men; and mixed with the scourings of all the washtubs, kennels and common sewers within the bills or mortality.

Sydney Smith commented, in the following century, 'There are a million insects in every drop', and this is confirmed by a pamphleteer who wrote at the time that Thames water was 'charged with the contents of more than 130 public common sewers, the drainings from the dung-hills and lay-stalls, the refuse of hospitals, slaughter-houses, colour, lead gas and soap works, drug-mills, and manufactures, and with all sorts of decomposed animal and vegetable substances, rendering the said water offensive and destructive to health.'

The huge sales of expensive bottled water today point to the fact that – although it is supposedly treated and filtered at pumping stations before being released into the system, tap water is not always pleasant or safe to drink. Nor is drawing it straight from a well any guarantee: a severe typhoid outbreak some years ago was caused by well water which a farmer used for washing his milk pails. His cows' milk was mixed with milk from other suppliers and delivered to a nearby seaside town where many people went down with typhoid. It turned out that the well had been contaminated by the septic tank at a nearby country house, which drained into a field. One of the guests staying at the house was a typhoid carrier.

Webbed Fingers and Toes

This is a congenital condition; sometimes, the toes or fingers are joined by a thin web of skin; otherwise, they may be fused together.

A successful London solicitor whose toes are webbed claims that he finds this very helpful if his yacht capsizes, like wearing a permanent pair of rubber flippers.

Weil's Disease

Also known as leptospirosis, this is an infection carried in the urine of rats. In its worst form it causes enlargement of the liver, inflammation of the kidneys, bleeding from the orifices and eventual death.

Although its most common victims are sewage workers, a well-known man of letters contracted it from bathing in his own swimming pool which the local rats use as a public lavatory. It is possible, however, that the enlargement of his liver may have had something to do with his daily consumption of alcohol.

Women (inflatable)
Troops for the use of

Among the lesser-known items of ordnance indented to the US Armed forces for use on active service abroad is a variety of life-size inflatable women, made of plastic or rubber. During the Vietnam War, three types were available to suit all basic tastes: one resembling Jackie Kennedy, another like Marilyn Monroe, while others preferred a Dorothy Dandridge look-alike. For use, these were pumped full of warm water and, perhaps saved a few men from the gonorrhea (*qv*) which rampaged through the troops.

Zits
See Acne

Zoonoses

Over a hundred and fifty diseases can be transmitted from animals and birds to man, and these are known collectively as Zoonoses. Brucellosis and bovine tuberculosis can be contracted from drinking untreated milk; hyatid cysts which grow to enormous size are caused by embryo tapeworm (*qv*) and ringworm (*qv*) which lodge in the liver and brain. Budgerigar fancier's lung and psittacosis are occupational hazards of people who keep caged birds. Perhaps the worst is rabies which is carried by wolves, foxes and vampire bats as well as by dogs. It causes madness in its host animal which rushes about, snapping and biting any creature it sees. In man, it causes inability to swallow food or drink; terror and convulsions; and a hacking cough which sounds eerily like a dog's bark. Death through exhaustion usually follows within a week of infection.

All Futura Books are available at your bookshop or newsagent, or can be ordered from the following address: Futura Books, Cash Sales Department, P.O. Box 11, Falmouth, Cornwall.

Please send cheque or postal order (no currency), and allow 55p for postage and packing for the first book plus 22p for the second book and 14p for each additional book ordered up to a maximum charge of £1.75 in U.K.

Customers in Eire and B.F.P.O. please allow 55p for the first book, 22p for the second book plus 14p per copy for the next 7 books, thereafter 8p per book.

Overseas customers please allow £1 for postage and packing for the first book and 25p per copy for each additional book.